SCHOLASTIC

National Curriculum
MATHS
Revision Guide

- ✓ Recap
- ✓ Revise
- ✓ Skills Check

Ages 7-8
Year 3

KS2

SCHOLASTIC

National Curriculum
MATHS
Revision Guide

Book End, Range Road, Witney, Oxfordshire, OX29 0YD
Registered office: Westfield Road, Southam, Warwickshire CV47 0RA
www.scholastic.co.uk

© 2016, Scholastic Ltd

56789 89012345

British Library Cataloguing-in-Publication Data
A catalogue record for this book is available from the British Library.

ISBN 978-1407-15987-4
Printed in Malaysia

Due to the nature of the web we cannot guarantee the content or links of
any site mentioned. We strongly recommend that teachers check websites
before using them in the classroom.

Every effort has been made to trace copyright holders for the works
reproduced in this book, and the publishers apologise for any inadvertent
omissions.

Author
Ann Montague-Smith

Consultant
Paul Hollin

Editorial
Rachel Morgan, Jenny Wilcox, Mark Walker, Red Door Media Ltd,
Christine Vaughan, Margaret Eaton, Janette Ratcliffe and Julia Roberts

Series Design
Scholastic Design Team: Nicolle Thomas and Neil Salt

Design
Oxford Designers & Illustrators

Cover Design
Scholastic Design Team: Nicolle Thomas and Neil Salt

Cover Illustration
Shutterstock / © VIGE.CO

Illustration
Tom Heard, The Bright Agency

Contents

Measurement

Geometry

Statistics

How to use this book

Introduction

This book has been written to help children reinforce the mathematics they have learned at school. It provides information and varied examples, activities and questions in a clear and consistent format across 39 units, covering all of National Curriculum for Mathematics for this age group.

I give tips to children and adults alike!

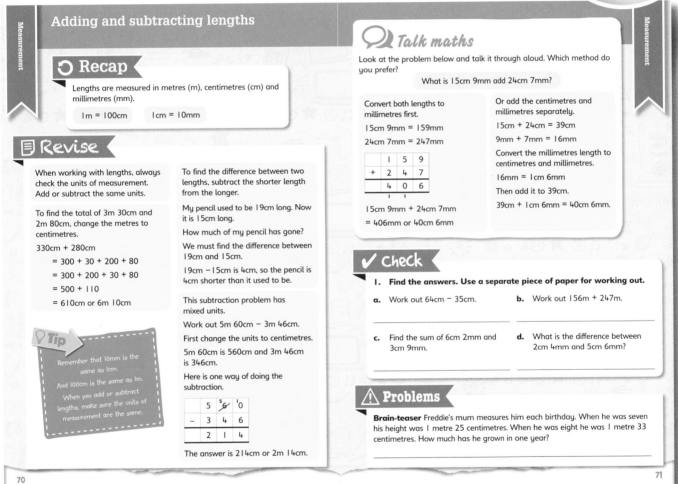

Adding and subtracting lengths

↻ Recap

Lengths are measured in metres (m), centimetres (cm) and millimetres (mm).

1m = 100cm   1cm = 10mm

目 Revise

When working with lengths, always check the units of measurement. Add or subtract the same units.

To find the total of 3m 30cm and 2m 80cm, change the metres to centimetres.

330cm + 280cm

= 300 + 30 + 200 + 80

= 300 + 200 + 30 + 80

= 500 + 110

= 610cm or 6m 10cm

Tip

Remember that 10mm is the same as 1cm.
And 100cm is the same as 1m.
When you add or subtract lengths, make sure the units of measurement are the same.

To find the difference between two lengths, subtract the shorter length from the longer.

My pencil used to be 19cm long. Now it is 15cm long.

How much of my pencil has gone?

We must find the difference between 19cm and 15cm.

19cm −15cm is 4cm, so the pencil is 4cm shorter than it used to be.

This subtraction problem has mixed units.

Work out 5m 60cm − 3m 46cm.

First change the units to centimetres.

5m 60cm is 560cm and 3m 46cm is 346cm.

Here is one way of doing the subtraction.

	5	⁵6	¹0
−	3	4	6
	2	1	4

The answer is 214cm or 2m 14cm.

💬 Talk maths

Look at the problem below and talk it through aloud. Which method do you prefer?

What is 15cm 9mm add 24cm 7mm?

Convert both lengths to millimetres first.

15cm 9mm = 159mm

24cm 7mm = 247mm

	1	5	9
+	2	4	7
	4	0	6

15cm 9mm + 24cm 7mm

= 406mm or 40cm 6mm

Or add the centimetres and millimetres separately.

15cm + 24cm = 39cm

9mm + 7mm = 16mm

Convert the millimetres length to centimetres and millimetres.

16mm = 1cm 6mm

Then add it to 39cm.

39cm + 1cm 6mm = 40cm 6mm.

✔ Check

1. **Find the answers. Use a separate piece of paper for working out.**

a. Work out 64cm − 35cm.

b. Work out 156m + 247m.

c. Find the sum of 6cm 2mm and 3cm 9mm.

d. What is the difference between 2cm 4mm and 5cm 6mm?

⚠ Problems

Brain-teaser Freddie's mum measures him each birthday. When he was seven his height was 1 metre 25 centimetres. When he was eight he was 1 metre 33 centimetres. How much has he grown in one year?

70   71

Unit structure

- **Recap** – a recap of basic facts of the mathematical area in focus.
- **Revise** – examples and facts specific to the age group.
- **Tips** – short and simple advice to aid understanding.
- **Talk maths** – focused activities that encourage verbal practice.
- **Check** – a focused range of questions, with answers at the end of the book.
- **Problems** – word problems requiring mathematics to be used in context.

Keep some blank or squared paper handy for notes and calculations!

Using this book at home

Improving your child's maths
It sounds obvious, but this is the best reason for using this book. Whether working sequentially through units, dipping in to resolve confusion, or reinforcing classroom learning, you can use this book to help your child see the benefits and pleasures of being competent in maths.

Consolidating school work
Most schools communicate clearly what they are doing each week via newsletters or homework. Using this book, alongside the maths being done at school, can boost children's mastery of the concepts.

Be sure not to get ahead of schoolwork or to confuse your child. If in doubt, talk to your child's class teacher.

Revising for tests
Regular testing is a fact of life for children these days, like it or not. Improving children's confidence is a good way to avoid stress as well as improve performance. Where children have obvious difficulties, dipping in to the book and focusing on specific facts and skills can be very helpful. To provide specific practice for end-of-year tests we recommend *National Curriculum Maths Tests for Year 3*.

Tips for effective home learning

Do a little, often
Keep sessions to an absolute maximum of 30 minutes. Even if children want to keep going, short amounts of focused study on a regular basis will help to sustain learning and enthusiasm in the long run.

Track progress
The revision tracker chart on page 7 provides a simple way for children to record their progress with this book. Remember, you've really 'got it' when you can understand and apply the maths confidently in different contexts. This means all the questions in the *Check* and *Problems* sections should not present any difficulties.

Avoid confusion
If your child really doesn't seem to understand a particular unit, take a step back. There may be some prior knowledge that s/he does not understand, or it may contradict how they have learned similar facts at school. Try looking at much simpler examples than those given in the book, and if in doubt talk to your child's teacher.

Talk, talk, talk
There is big value in discussing maths, both using vocabulary and explaining concepts. The more children can be encouraged to do this, especially explaining their thinking and understanding, the better the learning. Even if adults understand the work better than children, having them 'teach' you is a great way to consolidate their learning.

Practice makes perfect
Even the world's best footballers have to regularly practise kicking a ball. Brief warm ups before starting a unit, such as rapid recall of times tables or addition facts, or answering a few questions on mathematical vocabulary (see glossary) can help keep children on their toes.

Maths is everywhere – use it!
Children have lots of English lessons at school, and they use language almost constantly in daily life. They also have lots of maths lessons but encounter its use in daily life much less. Involving children in everyday maths is very useful. Shopping and money are the obvious ones, but cooking, decorating, planning holidays, catching buses, to name a few examples, can all involve important mathematical thinking and talk.

Revision tracker

	Not sure	Getting there	Got it!
Count in steps of 4 and 8, and 50 and 100			
Read, write, order and compare 3-digit numbers in numerals and words			
Say what each digit in a 3-digit number means			
Find 10 or 100 more or less than a 3-digit number			
Identify a number pattern, continue the pattern, and find missing numbers			
Solve number problems			
Use mental methods to add and subtract			
Use formal written methods to add			
Use formal written methods to subtract			
Estimate and check an addition or subtraction calculation			
Solve addition and subtraction problems			
Use multiplication facts that I know to find related division facts			
Use mental methods for multiplication and division			
Use written methods for multiplication and division			
Solve multiplication and division problems			
Find tenths of objects and numbers			
Find fractions of objects			
Find fractions of numbers			
Find and recognise equivalent fractions			
Compare and order fractions			
Add and subtract fractions with the same denominator			
Solve fraction problems			
Measure and compare length			
Measure and compare mass			
Measure and compare capacity and volume			
Tell and write the time from an analogue clock			
Tell and write the time from a Roman numeral clock			
Tell and write the time using 24-hour clocks			
Use the vocabulary of time			
Say how many days there are in each month, year and leap year			
Calculate how long an event takes			
Find the perimeter of 2D shapes			
Add and subtract amounts of money and find change			
Add and subtract lengths			
Add and subtract mass			
Add and subtract volume and capacity			
Identify horizontal, vertical, perpendicular and parallel lines			
Draw 2D shapes with reasonable accuracy			
Recognise and name 3D shapes and make models of them			
Recognise that angles are a property of shape or a description of a turn			
Identify right angles, make and recognise right angled turns, and identify whether angles are greater or less than a right angle			
Interpret and present data using tables and pictograms			
Solve two-step questions using information from tables and pictograms			
Interpret and present data using tables and bar charts			
Solve two-step questions using information from tables and bar charts			

Counting in multiples

↻ Recap

You can count in multiples of 5 and 10 on a number line.

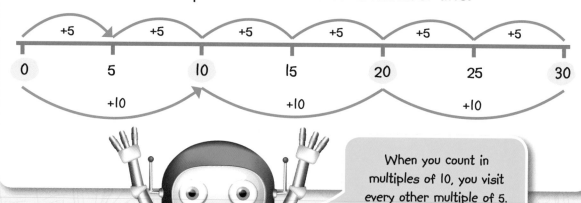

When you count in multiples of 10, you visit every other multiple of 5.

📄 Revise

You can also count in multiples of 4 and 8 on a number line.

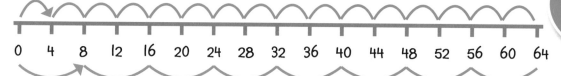

Every other multiple of 4 is also a multiple of 8.

Look carefully at the two counts. What do you notice?

This number line shows how we count in multiples of 50 and 100.

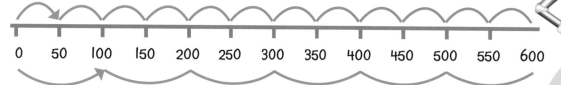

What do you notice about these two counts?

Every other multiple of 50 is also a multiple of 100.

Hello! Here are some tips on multiples!

💡 Tips

Double a multiple of 4 to find the multiple of 8.

$6 \times 4 = 24$

$6 \times 8 = 48$

Double a multiple of 50 to find the multiple of 100.

$4 \times 50 = 200$

$4 \times 100 = 400$

💬 Talk maths

Read these counts out loud.

Count in 4s.

0, 4, 8, 12, 16, 20, 24, 28, 32, 36, 40, 44, 48, 52

Count in 8s.

0, 8, 16, 24, 32, 40, 48, 56, 64, 72, 80, 88, 96

Count in 100s.

0, 100, 200, 300, 400, 500, 600, 700, 800, 900, 1000

And in 50s.

0, 50, 100, 150, 200, 250, 300, 350, 400, 450, 500

DID YOU KNOW?

Did you know that you can count in thousands in the same way? 0, 1000, 2000, 3000, 4000, 5000

✔ Check

Write the missing numbers in these counts.

1. 8, 12, _____, 20, _____, _____, _____

2. 16, 24, _____, _____, _____, 56, _____

3. 150, 200, 250, _____, _____, _____

4. 300, 400, _____, _____, _____, _____, 900

5. 1000, 900, 800, _____, _____, _____, _____

⚠ Problems

Brain-teaser Sally writes all the multiples of 50, from 0 to 600.

Which numbers does she write?

_____

Brain-buster Jon counts in 4s. Paul counts in 8s.

They both start on 16 and they finish on 48.

Which numbers do they both say?

_____

Numbers to 1000

↻ Recap

Here is a 2-digit number.

tens	ones
7	2

The 7 represents 7 tens. The 2 represents 2 ones.
This makes 72.

📄 Revise

Look at this 3-digit number.

The first digit tells you how many hundreds.

The second digit tells you how many tens.

The third digit tells you how many ones.

To compare two numbers, look at the hundreds digit in each number first.

hundreds   tens   ones

456

Read this statement aloud. For the symbol > say *is bigger than*.

654 > 456 because 6 > 4

If the hundreds digits are the same, look at the tens digit.

Read this statement aloud. For the symbol < say *is smaller than*.

325 < 381 because 2 < 8

We can compare more than two numbers in the same way and put them in order.

For example, 456 < 546 and 546 < 645, so 456 < 546 < 645.

When you read numbers in words, remember to think about place value. If a number has no tens, or no ones, you need to write a zero.

We write two hundred and six as 206.

Tips 💡

Remember to check the hundreds digit first when comparing numbers. Then check the tens, then the ones.

If you get mixed up with the > and < symbols just think of the symbol as the mouth of a crocodile – the crocodile always eats the bigger number!

654 > 456 <

 Talk maths

Say these numbers in order. Start with the smallest.

312   516   499   844   484   488

Now read these numbers.

four hundred and thirteen

six hundred and forty-seven

nine hundred and ninety

- Which number has the smallest tens?
- Which number has the largest ones?
- Which number is closest to one thousand?

✔ Check

1. **Write these numbers in digits.**

   a. three hundred and sixty-five _____

   b. two hundred and fifteen _____

2. **Now write these numbers in words.**

   a. 804   **b.** 970

   _____   _____

3. **Write these numbers in order, starting with the smallest.**

   735   573   537   753   357 _____

4. **Use < or > to compare these pairs of numbers.**

   321 _____ 243   645 _____ 654   720 _____ 702

⚠ Problems

Brain-buster Sally makes four piles of swap cards. The first pile has 425 cards, the second pile has 245 cards, the third pile has 542 cards and the fourth pile has 524 cards. Write the number of cards in each pile in size order, starting with the smallest.

_____

Place value

↺ Recap

This number is made from 4 hundreds and 2 tens and 6 ones.

hundreds	tens	ones
4	2	6

📋 Revise

Here is a number square.

301	302	303	304	305	306	307	308	309	310
311	312	313	314	315	316	317	318	319	320
321	322	323	324	325	326	327	328	329	330
331	332	333	334	335	336	337	338	339	340
341	342	343	344	345	346	347	348	349	350
351	352	353	354	355	356	357	358	359	360
361	362	363	364	365	366	367	368	369	370
371	372	373	374	375	376	377	378	379	380
381	382	383	384	385	386	387	388	389	390
391	392	393	394	395	396	397	398	399	400

Look carefully at the numbers in the number square.

All the numbers in each column have the same ones digit. Look at the third column. All the numbers have 3 as their ones digit.

All the numbers in each row have the same tens digit. Look at the fifth row. All the numbers have 4 as their tens digit.

Find 356 in the number square.

356 has 3 hundreds and 5 tens and 6 ones.

So 356 can be partitioned like this:
356 = 300 + 50 + 6

We can also partition 356 like this:
356 = 200 + 150 + 6

Can you think of another way to partition 356?

 Talk maths

Say these numbers aloud.

What does each number represent?

How could you partition them?

Which number is the largest?

365

374

273

408

✔ Check

1. Write in digits the number with five hundreds and six tens and seven ones.

    _____

2. A number can be partitioned like this: 300 + 270 + 6. Write the number in digits.

    _____

3. A number can be partitioned like this: six hundred + two hundred and forty + sixteen. Write the number in digits.

    _____

4. Partition the number 379.

    _____

⚠ Problems

Brain-teaser In a shop there are 300 red pens, 130 blue pens and six black pens. How many pens are there altogether?

_____

Brain-buster The shopkeeper also sells pencils. Yesterday he counted 200 black pencils, 250 green pencils and there were no red pencils. Then he sold 25 green pencils. How many pencils does the shopkeeper have now?

_____

Finding 10 or 100 more or less

↺ Recap

One less than 325 is 324. One more than 325 is 326.

When we add or subtract 1, the ones digit changes.

hundreds	tens	ones
3	2	4

one less

←

hundreds	tens	ones
3	2	5

→

hundreds	tens	ones
3	2	6

one more

📋 Revise

When we add or subtract 10, it is the tens digit that changes.

tens	ones
3	5

ten less

←

tens	ones
4	5

→

tens	ones
5	5

ten more

Ten less than 45 is 35. Ten more than 45 is 55.

hundreds	tens	ones
3	7	5

ten less

←

hundreds	tens	ones
3	8	5

→

hundreds	tens	ones
3	9	5

ten more

When we add or subtract 100, it is the hundreds digit that changes.

hundreds	tens	ones
2	8	5

one hundred less

←

hundreds	tens	ones
3	8	5

→

hundreds	tens	ones
4	8	5

one hundred more

💡 Tip

Sometimes adding or subtracting 10 affects the hundreds digit.

596   ten more → $596 + 10 = 500 + 90 + 10 + 6 = 500 + 100 + 6 = 606$

506   ten less → $506 - 10 = 400 + 100 - 10 + 6 = 400 + 90 + 6 = 496$

💬 Talk Maths

Say aloud what is ten more than each number.

Say aloud what is ten less than each number.

Say aloud what is thirty more than each number.

Say what is one hundred more or less than each number.

How did you work it out?

777

503

491

665

✔ Check

Write the number that is:

1. ten more than 523.

_____

2. ten less than 601.

_____

3. one hundred more than 750.

_____

4. one hundred less than 532.

_____

5. eighty more than 246.

_____

6. ninety less than 139.

_____

⚠ Problems

Brain-teaser Nick has £493 in his savings bank. He gives Simon £100. How much money does Nick have now?

_____

Brain-buster Katie counts how much money she has. There is £507 in her savings account. She gives Noah £100. Then she gives Noah another £10. How much money does Katie have now?

_____

Number patterns

↺ Recap

You should recognise this number pattern.

15   20   25   30

These are multiples of 5. Each number is five more than the previous number.

In this number pattern, the numbers get smaller.

28   24   20   16

These are multiples of 4. Each number is four less than the previous number.

What are the next three numbers in the pattern?

📄 Revise

Look at the number pattern on the hundred square.

Look at the shaded numbers. Each number is eight more than the previous number. So we can add 8 to find the next three numbers in the pattern.

64 + 8 = 72, 72 + 8 = 80, 80 + 8 = 88

You can use a number line to help you count on.

Look at this number pattern.

38   42   46   ★   ★   ★

Each number is four more than the previous number.

1	2	3	4	5	6	7	8	9	10
11	12	13	14	15	16	17	18	19	20
21	22	23	24	25	26	27	28	29	30
31	32	33	34	35	36	37	38	39	40
41	42	43	44	45	46	47	48	49	50
51	52	53	54	55	56	57	58	59	60
61	62	63	64	65	66	67	68	69	70
71	72	73	74	75	76	77	78	79	80
81	82	83	84	85	86	87	88	89	90
91	92	93	94	95	96	97	98	99	100

+4   +4   +4   +4

38   42   46   50   54

💡 Tip

Use whichever tool you find most helpful – a number square or a number line. You can count along the rows or down the columns of a number square to look for number patterns.

Number patterns are fun but tricky! Maybe I can help.

💬 Talk maths

Read these number patterns aloud. What do you need to add to find the next number? Say the missing numbers.

45   50   55   60   65   ★   ★   ★

25   22   19   ★   ★   ★   7   4

What do you notice about the numbers?

Find the mistake in this pattern. Say the correct pattern.

19   23   27   30   35   39

Explain to a friend or adult how you found the mistake.

One number is missing from this pattern. Say the correct pattern.

100   104   108   116   120   124

✔ Check

1. Write the next three numbers in these patterns.

a.   5, 45, 85, _____

b.   150, 200, 250, _____

c.   97, 87, 77, _____

2. There is a mistake or missing number in each of these patterns. Write the pattern correctly.

a.   11, 14, 17, 23, 26, 29

_____

b.   96, 90, 84, 80, 74, 68

_____

⚠ Problems

Brain-teaser Tom drew a number line, starting at 46. He counted on 3, and wrote the number. He did this five more times. What numbers did he write?

_____

Brain-buster David drew a number line and wrote 24 at the beginning of the line. Then he counted on 5 and wrote the number. He did that another ten times.

Paul drew a number line and wrote 14 at the beginning. Then he counted on 10 and wrote that number. He did this another six times.

Which numbers did both boys write on their number lines?

_____

17

Solving number problems

↻ Recap

You can use the skills you have revised so far to help you solve word problems.

📋 Revise

This question asks you to count on. You can draw a number line to help you.

Sam counts on from 5 in tens six times. What numbers does she say?

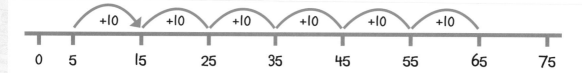

Look at this problem:

Tim goes shopping. He wants to buy a new tablet computer.

Which shop has the cheapest price?

First work out the price of the computer at each shop.

Buy Me Cheap:	£455 − £100 = £355
Computer Express:	£365 − £10 = £355
Geeks Rule:	£440 − £100 = £340

Then compare the prices.

£340 < £355 so Geeks Rule is the cheapest.

Need help with number problems? No problem!

Tips

Make sure you show your working with problems like these so that others can see how you thought through the problem.

Don't panic when you see a lot of words! Read the question slowly and write down the calculations you need to do.

💬 *Talk maths*

How would you solve these problems? Talk through them with a friend or adult and explain how you know the answers

Jan has 567 sheep on her farm. Then she has another 100 lambs. How many is that in total?

Paul has £157. His grandfather gives him another £10. Then Paul spends £100. How much money does he have now?

✔ Check

Answer these questions. Write down your working out.

If there are units of measurement in the question, remember to write the units in your answer.

1. James measures some rope. It is 659cm long. He cuts off 100cm. How much rope does he have left?

2. There are 650 litres of water in a tank. 100 litres are poured out. Then 10 litres are added to the tank. How much water is in the tank now?

3. The sand in the blue sand timer runs through in 180 seconds. The sand in the red sand timer runs through 10 seconds slower than the blue sand timer. How long does the red sand timer take?

⚠ Problems

Brain-teaser There are 640 children in the school. 100 of the children will leave in July. Another 10 children will come to the school in September. How many children will there be at the school in September?

Brain-buster Dilshad writes the digits 579. He makes as many different numbers from these three digits as he can. What is the largest number he can make?

Mental methods for addition and subtraction

↻ Recap

You can use a mental number line to add or subtract. For example, to add 47 and 6, count on 6 from 47: 48, 49, 50, 51, 52, 53.

Sometimes it helps to break up the number you are adding or subtracting. For example, for 52 − 8, you can think of 8 as 2 + 6. Subtract the 2, then the 6. So 52 − 8 = 52 − 2 − 6 = 50 − 6.

Revise

To add a 1-digit number to a 3-digit number, add enough ones to make the next ten, then add on the rest of the ones.

326 + 7 = 326 + 4 + 3 = 330 + 3 = 333

You can do the same to subtract. Subtract enough ones to leave 0 ones, then subtract the rest of the ones.

423 − 8 = 423 − 3 − 5 = 420 − 5 = 415

Or you could subtract 10 and then adjust the answer. For example, instead of subtracting 8, you could subtract 10 and then add 2.

423 − 8 = 423 − 10 + 2 = 413 + 2 = 415

To add tens to a 3-digit number, add the two tens digits together.

427 + 30 = 420 + 30 + 7 = 450 + 7 = 457

Or count on three tens from 427 : 437, 447, 457

To subtract, take away the tens and then add the ones back.

527 − 30 = 520 − 30 + 7 = 400 + 120 − 30 + 7 = 400 + 90 + 7 = 497

Or count back three tens from 527 : 517, 507, 497

To add hundreds to a 3-digit number, add the two hundreds digits together.

438 + 300 = 400 + 300 + 38 = 700 + 38 = 738

Or count on three hundreds from 438 : 538, 638, 738

To subtract, take away the hundreds and then add the tens and ones back.

927 − 400 = 900 − 400 + 27 = 500 + 27 = 527

Or count back four hundreds from 927 : 827, 727, 627, 527

💬 Talk maths

Talk through these additions and subtractions with a friend or adult.
Make sure you understand them.

456 + 3 You know that 6 + 3 = 9 so 456 + 3 = 459.

527 − 3 You know that 7 − 3 = 4 so 527 − 3 = 524.

222 + 80 Add 20 and 80 to make 100.

So 222 + 80 = 200 + 100 + 2 = 302.

516 − 60 Try this: 516 − 10 − 50 = 506 − 50 = 456.

451 + 300 Here just add the hundreds digits. So that makes 751.

621 − 400 Take away the 4 hundreds from 6 hundreds. This leaves 221.

This is slightly trickier.

✔ Check

Think about the best way for you to solve these mentally, then write the answers.

1. 392 + 5

_____

2. 747 − 8

_____

3. 391 + 40

_____

4. 503 + 40

_____

5. 321 + 200

_____

6. 654 − 300

_____

⚠ Problems

Brain-teaser Peter has £652 in the bank. His grandfather gives him another £50. How much money does he have now?

_____

Brain-buster Megan has £205 to spend. She buys an MP3 player for £40 and an album for £6. How much money does Megan have now?

_____

Formal written addition methods

↻ Recap

You can add 2-digit numbers by adding the tens and ones separately.

Here is one way to work out 64 + 35.

60 + 4 + 30 + 5
= 90 + 9
= 99

This is a more formal method.

	60	+	4
+	30	+	5
	90	+	9

So 64 + 35 = 99

Here is another way.

	6	4
+	3	5
	9	9

Sometimes the ones total more than 10. Here are two ways of working out 57 + 29.

	50	+	7
+	20	+	9
	70	+	16
		86	

	5	7
+	2	9
	8	6
	₁	

▤ Revise

You can use the same methods to add 3-digit numbers.
Here are two ways of working out 135 + 287.

	100	+	30	+	5
+	200	+	80	+	7
	300	+	110	+	12
		410		+	12
			422		

	1	3	5
+	2	8	7
	4	2	2
		₁	₁

Carry 10s and 100s over by putting a small one under the line. Remember to add it on.

Tips

Try all the different methods several times before you decide which you like best.

Set out your work carefully, using squared paper to help you if possible. This will help you to line up the hundreds, tens and ones.

💬 Talk maths

Here are three formal additions. Explain what is happening in each one.

26 + 38

	2	6
+	3	8
	6	4
		1

156 + 47

	1	5	6
+		4	7
		1	3
		9	0
	1	0	3
	2	0	3
		1	

564 + 297

	5	6	4
+	2	9	7
		1	1
	1	5	0
	7	0	0
	8	6	1

Would you have used a different written method to work out these additions? Explain your choice to a friend or adult.

✔ Check

Use a formal written method for each of these.

1. 56 + 47

2. 145 + 37

3. 468 + 259

⚠ Problems

Brain-teaser There are 156 sweets in a jar. The shopkeeper pours into the jar another 48 sweets. How many sweets are there altogether?

_____

Brain-buster In one sweet jar there are 451 dolly mixtures. In another sweet jar there are 370 jelly babies. A child buys 30 dolly mixtures and 40 jelly babies. How many dolly mixtures and jelly babies are there now in total?

_____

Formal written subtraction methods

↺ Recap

You can use a formal written method to subtract, too.

$$
\begin{array}{r}
90 + 4 \\
- \quad 30 + 3 \\
\hline
60 + 1 \\
\hline
\end{array}
\qquad
\begin{array}{r}
9 \quad 4 \\
- \quad 3 \quad 3 \\
\hline
6 \quad 1 \\
\hline
\end{array}
$$

So 94 − 33 = 61

📄 Revise

If there are not enough ones you will need to partition the tens number.

Here are two ways of working out 85 − 37.

$$
\begin{array}{r}
80 + 5 \\
- \quad 30 + 7 \\
\hline
70 + 15 \\
- \quad 30 + 7 \\
\hline
40 + 8 \\
\hline
48 \\
\end{array}
$$

$$
\begin{array}{r}
{}^{70}\!\!\!\not{80} + {}^{1}5 \\
- \quad 30 + 7 \\
\hline
40 + 8 \\
\hline
48 \\
\end{array}
$$

You can use the same method to subtract a 2-digit number from a 3-digit number. Here is one way of working out 253 − 36.

$$
\begin{array}{r}
200 + 50 + 3 \; = \\
- \qquad\;\; 30 + 6 \; = \\
\hline
\end{array}
\qquad
\begin{array}{r}
200 + 40 + 13 \\
-\qquad\; 30 + 6 \\
\hline
200 + 10 + 7 \; = \; 217 \\
\end{array}
$$

When you subtract a 3-digit number from a 3-digit number, sometimes you need to partition both the tens number and the hundreds number.

Here are two ways of working out 341 − 196.

$$
\begin{array}{r}
{}^{200}\!\!\!\not{300} + {}^{130}\!\!\!\not{40} + {}^{1}1 \\
- \quad 100 + 90 + 6 \\
\hline
200 + 130 + 11 \\
- \quad 100 + 90 + 6 \\
\hline
100 + 40 + 5 \\
\hline
145 \\
\end{array}
$$

$$
\begin{array}{r}
{}^{2}\!\!\not{3}\;{}^{13}\!\!\not{4}\;{}^{1}1 \\
- \; 1\;\;9\;\;6 \\
\hline
1\;\;4\;\;5 \\
\hline
\end{array}
$$

💬 Talk maths

Talk through these subtractions with a friend or adult. Explain each step.

You need to exchange a ten for ones.

64 − 32

	6	4
−	3	2
	3	2

95 − 68

	⁸9̸	¹5
−	6	8
	2	7

In these examples you need to exchange a hundred for 10 tens, and then exchange one of those tens for 10 ones.

327 − 59

	²3̸	¹¹2̸	¹7
−		5	9
	2	6	8

645 − 379

	⁵6̸	¹³4̸	¹5
−	3	7	9
	2	6	6

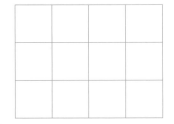

✔ Check

Use a formal written method for each of these.

I. 84 − 31

2. 237 − 59

3. 666 − 478

⚠ Problems

Brain-teaser A farmer counts how many eggs the chickens have laid. He counts 427. He sells 59 eggs. How many eggs are left?

_____

Brain-buster There are 728 eggs in their boxes. The farmer sells 150 on Monday, and 275 on Tuesday. How many eggs are left?

_____

Estimating and using inverses

⟳ Recap

You know how to add and subtract a 2-digit number and a tens number.

$$24 + 40 = 64$$
$$36 - 20 = 16$$

Revise

When you do a calculation, estimate the answer first so you can check your actual answer is about right. Look at the numbers and think of numbers that are close to them that are easier to work out.

For example, for $64 + 12$ you could estimate $60 + 10 = 70$.

Using inverses

Addition is the inverse (or opposite) of subtraction.

Subtraction is the inverse (or opposite) of addition.

This means we can use subtraction to check the answer to an addition or we can use addition to check the answer to a subtraction.

An good estimate for $156 + 58$ is $160 + 60 = 220$.

Here is one way of working out $156 + 58$.

	1	5	6
+		5	8
	2	1	4

Check with subtraction.

	²1̸	¹⁰0̸	¹4
−		5	8
	1	5	6

We have 156, 58 and 214 in both calculations.

214 is just a bit smaller than 220 so our estimate helps us to check we are about right.

For subtraction, check with addition.

This is a good estimate. The exact answer will be a bit larger than 70.

Don't just guess – estimate, calculate, check!

Tips 💡

Your answer should be close to your estimate. If it's not, look and see if you made a mistake in your calculation.

Use the inverse to check your answer – if the three numbers are not the same, do the calculation again.

 Talk maths

Don't forget:
Estimate. Calculate.
Check.

Talk about these estimates with a friend or adult.

Which are good estimates? How do you know?

| 64 + 72 | Estimate about 130 |
| 136 − 45 | Estimate about 100 |

| 75 + 38 | Estimate about 110 |
| 169 − 130 | Estimate about 30 |

✔ Check

Estimate the answer to each calculation. Use the formal written method you like best. Use inverse calculations to check your answers.

1. 56 + 39

2. 92 − 44

3. 222 + 468

4. 143 − 76

5. 356 + 47

6. 596 − 217

⚠ Problems

Brain-teaser A shop has 351 metres of blue ribbon. The shop assistant sells 94 metres of the ribbon. What length of ribbon is left?

Brain-buster Some volunteers are going to plant 431 young trees in a wood. On the first day they plant 96 trees and on the second day they plant 29 trees. How many trees still need to be planted?

Solving addition and subtraction problems

↻ Recap

You can use the addition and subtraction methods you have learned so far to help you solve problems.

📄 Revise

You can solve missing number problems like this by counting up.

$35 + ★ = 44$

Count on from 35: 35 and 5 is 40. Another 4 is 44.

$5 + 4 = 9$, so the missing number is 9.

Can you think of another way to solve this problem?

This missing number problem has larger numbers.

$47 + ★ = 116$

You can still count on to solve it.

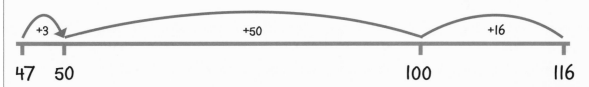

47 50   100   116

$3 + 50 + 16 = 69$, so the missing number is 69.

You can also solve the problem with a subtraction sentence.

$116 - 47 = 100 - 40 + 16 - 7 = 60 + 9 = 69$

Don't let problems cause you problems! Take them one step at a time.

If you prefer, you can use a formal written method.

This missing problem involves subtraction.

$237 - ★ = 156$

Count on from 156 to 237 to find the missing number.

156 160   200   237

$4 + 40 + 37 = 81$, so the missing number is 81.

Or you can subtract 156 from 237 to find the missing number.

💬 Talk maths

How would you solve these problems? Explain to a friend or adult what you know and what you need to work out. How many ways can you think of to find the answer?

Find the missing number.

59 + ★ = 153

★ − 92 = 200

Jon has 256 marbles. He gives some to Mark. Now Jon has only 185 marbles. How many marbles does Mark have?

Can you write this as a missing number problem?

✔ Check

Solve each missing number problem.

1. 94 + _____ = 165

2. _____ + 89 = 200

3. _____ + 66 = 100

4. 174 − _____ = 36

5. The difference between 156 and 251 is _____

⚠ Problems

Brain-teaser Travis has £98 in his money box. He buys a guitar and now he has £65 in his money box. How much did the guitar cost?

_____

Brain-buster Lexi buys her mother a bunch of flowers for £33, a box of chocolates for £17 and a special card for £8. Now she has £74 left. How much money did Lexi have to begin with?

_____

3, 4 and 8 multiplication and division facts

↺ Recap

You already know the multiplication facts for 2, 5 and 10.
Look at the table below and check you remember them.

📄 Revise

You need to learn the multiplication for facts 3, 4 and 8.

Remember, if you know $3 \times 4 = 12$, you also know $4 \times 3 = 12$.

You can use multiplication facts to find division facts.

If you know $4 \times 3 = 12$ and $3 \times 4 = 12$, you also know $12 \div 3 = 4$

and $12 \div 4 = 3$.

×	1	2	3	4	5	6	7	8	9	10	11	12
2	2	4	6	8	10	12	14	16	18	20	22	24
3	3	6	9	12	15	18	21	24	27	30	33	36
4	4	8	12	16	20	24	28	32	36	40	44	48
5	5	10	15	20	25	30	35	40	45	50	55	60
8	8	16	24	32	40	48	56	64	72	80	88	96
10	10	20	30	40	50	60	70	80	90	100	110	120

💡 Tips

You can multiply numbers in any order.

If you know a multiplication fact, you can work out a division fact.

If you forget a multiplication fact, you can sometimes use doubling to help you. For example, to find 7 × 8, work out 7 × 4 and double the answer.

You know more facts than you think you do!

 Talk maths

Ask a friend or adult to test you on your multiplication facts.

Circle the multiplication facts you know in the table.

Can you think of ways to remember the ones you are not sure of?

✔ Check

Cover up the table with a piece of paper.

Write down the answers to these using your memory.

1. 9 × 8 = _____

2. 44 ÷ 4 = _____

3. 96 ÷ 8 = _____

4. 9 × 3 = _____

5. 36 ÷ 3 = _____

6. 4 × 12 = _____

⚠ Problems

Brain-teaser Maia has 24 sweets to be shared between herself and three friends. How many sweets do they each get?

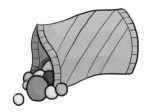

_____

Brain-buster There are 48 pencils to be shared out equally into pots. Each pot contains six pencils. How many pots are there?

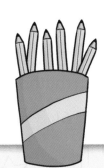

_____

Using mental and written methods for multiplication and division

📄 Revise

You can use your multiplication tables to work out 2-digit by 1-digit multiplications. Here are four different ways of working out 16 × 4.

You can write a multiplication sentence.

16 × 4 = 10 × 4 + 6 × 4 = 40 + 24 = 64

	10 × 4		6 × 4	
0		40		64

You can use the grid method.

×	4
10	40
6	24
Total	64

You can use a formal written method.

	1	6
×		4
	2	4	Multiply the ones
	4	0	Multiply the tens.
	6	4

You can also break a division down into sections.
Here are two ways of working out 64 ÷ 4.

This is the division sentence method.

64 ÷ 4   = 40 ÷ 4 + 24 ÷ 4
           = 10 + 6
           = 16

This method is called chunking.

	6	4	
−	4	0	10 × 4
	2	4	
−	2	4	6 × 4
		0	16

So 64 ÷ 4 = 16

 Talk maths

Look at the division below and talk through both methods aloud, saying how each stage was done. Which do you find easier?

$$54 \div 3$$

Division sentence method

$54 \div 3 \quad = 30 \div 3 + 24 \div 3$

$\qquad\qquad = 10 + 8$

$\qquad\qquad = 18$

Chunking method

	5	4	
−	3	0	10 × 3
	2	4	
−	2	4	8 × 3
		0	18 So 54 ÷ 3 = 18

✔ Check

Use a written method to solve these.

Choose the method that you feel most confident with.

1. 23 × 3   **2.** 68 ÷ 4   **3.** 96 ÷ 3   **4.** 96 ÷ 4

   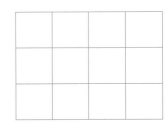

5. What is the product of 23 and 4? _____

⚠ Problems

Brain-teaser Ben has 88cm of string. He wants to divide it equally into four lengths. How much will there be in each length of string?

_____

Brain-buster Sally buys three pens. Each pen costs 31p. How much change will Sally have from £1?

_____

Solving multiplication and division problems

↻ Recap

You can use multiplication and division skills to solve problems.

Remember, if you know one fact, you also know three more facts.

| $5 \times 9 = 45$ | $9 \times 5 = 45$ | $45 \div 5 = 9$ | $45 \div 9 = 5$ |

📄 Revise

Here is a missing number problem.

$$\star \div 3 = 16$$

Decide what you need to work out.

What number, divided by 3, gives 16?

The answer must be 3 times bigger than 16.

So you need to work out 16×3.

		1	6
×			3
		3	0
		1	8
		4	8

You can use a grid to help you answer some types of question.

Steve has four T-shirts and three pairs of jeans. How many different outfits can he make? The grid shows all the different possibilities.

	T-shirt 1	T-shirt 2	T-shirt 3	T-shirt 4
Jeans 1	✔	✔	✔	✔
Jeans 2	✔	✔	✔	✔
Jeans 3	✔	✔	✔	✔

Steve has 12 possible outfits.

Work out 4×3. What do you notice?

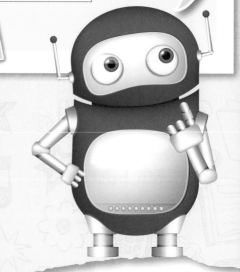

Tips 💡

Look for the numbers in the question. What do you need to do with them?

If you are not sure what to multiply or divide, think about what size the numbers should be.

$\star \div 3 = 16$ Multiply or divide?

$\star$ must be bigger than 16. Three times bigger, in fact.

So $3 \times 16 = \star$.

🗨 *Talk maths*

Look at the problem below. Talk through the answers aloud. Explain where the numbers in the answers come from.

> A cake for two people needs these ingredients.
>
> How much flour, sugar, butter and egg would be needed to make a cake for six people?

> 100g of flour
> 100g of sugar
> 100g of butter
> 2 eggs

6 ÷ 2 = 3 so you need three times as much of each ingredient to make a cake for six people.

Multiply each ingredient by 3.

100 × 3 = 300g of flour, 300g of sugar, 300g of butter

2 × 3 = 6 eggs

✔ Check

Find the missing numbers.

1. ★ × 8 = 104 **2.** ★ ÷ 4 = 15 **3.** 8 × ★ = 120 **4.** 52 ÷ ★ = 13

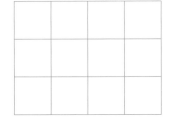 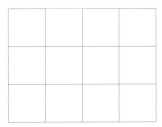 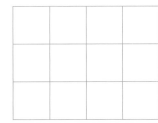 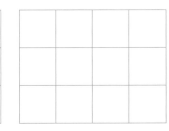

5. The product of 26 and 3 is _____.

⚠ Problems

Brain-buster Tim buys 32 small cartons of juice, for each guest at a party. He also buys 64 snack packs. Then he discovers that three times as many people will be coming to the party. How many more cartons of juice and snack packs does Tim need to buy?

_____

Tenths

↺ Recap

A fraction is made by dividing something into equal parts.

This cake has been divided into quarters.

Each slice is $\frac{1}{4}$ of the cake.

If one slice is eaten then $\frac{3}{4}$ is left.

Can you think of another fraction to describe the green squares?

📄 Revise

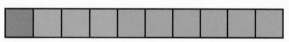

To find a tenth, divide squares or numbers by 10.

There are 10 squares in total.

1 out of 10 squares is red. $\frac{1}{10}$ is red.

3 out of 10 squares are blue. $\frac{3}{10}$ is blue.

6 out of 10 squares are green. $\frac{6}{10}$ is green.

10 out of 10 squares are coloured. $\frac{10}{10}$ is equivalent to one whole.

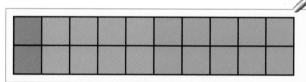

There are 20 squares in total.

$20 \div 10 = 2$. So two squares make $\frac{1}{10}$ of 20.

$\frac{1}{10}$ is red. $\frac{4}{10}$ are blue. $\frac{5}{10}$ are green.

💡 Tip

To find more than one tenth of a number, divide by 10 and then multiply.

$\frac{1}{10}$ of 20 is $20 \div 10 = 2$, so

$\frac{2}{10}$ of 20 is $2 \times 2 = 4$

$\frac{3}{10}$ of 20 is $2 \times 3 = 6$

$\frac{4}{10}$ of 20 is $2 \times 4 = 8$ and so on.

💬 Talk maths

Look at these problems. Talk through the answers aloud.

How do you know that one tenth of 40 is 4?

How can you work out three tenths of 90?

Kelso had 60 apples but gave $\frac{2}{10}$ to her gran. Kelso's gran received 12 apples. Is this correct?

✔ Check

Answer these questions.

1. $\frac{1}{10}$ of 30 = _____

2. $\frac{5}{10}$ of 100 = _____

3. $\frac{8}{10}$ of 50 = _____

4. $\frac{6}{10}$ of 30 = _____

5. $\frac{9}{10}$ of 20 = _____

6. $\frac{3}{10}$ of 40 = _____

⚠ Problems

Brain-teaser Jon has 30 marbles. He gives Charlie $\frac{7}{10}$ of his marbles. How many marbles does Charlie receive?

_____

Brain-buster Daisy the cow produces 30 litres of milk a day. $\frac{1}{10}$ of this milk is kept for the calves to drink. The farmer's wife keeps $\frac{2}{10}$ for herself and $\frac{3}{10}$ is kept for making butter. The rest is turned into cheese. How much milk in litres is used for making cheese?

_____

Fractions of objects

↺ Recap

The top number (numerator) tells us how many of the equal parts there are. Here there is 1 out of 5.

The bottom number (denominator) tells us how many equal parts there are in total. Here there are 5.

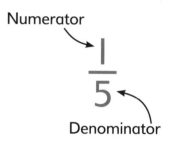

Numerator

$\dfrac{1}{5}$

Denominator

Revise

To find a fraction of a set of objects, divide the objects into equal groups.

Here are 16 balls.

To find $\frac{1}{2}$, divide the balls into two equal groups.

There are eight balls in each group.

$\frac{1}{2}$ of 16 is 8.

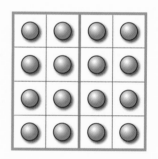

Here are the same 16 balls.

To find $\frac{1}{4}$, divide the balls into four equal groups.

There are four balls in each group.

$\frac{1}{4}$ of 16 is 4.

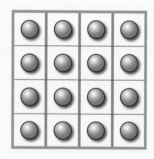

Here are the 16 balls again.

To find $\frac{3}{4}$, divide the balls into four equal groups, then count the balls in three of the groups.

$\frac{3}{4}$ of 16 is 12.

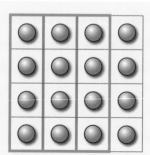

Talk maths

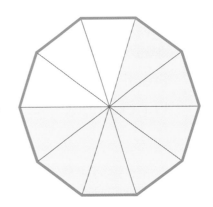

Discuss aloud the fractions shown.

Explain how you know.

✔ Check

Use squared paper to help you.

1. $\frac{1}{8}$ of 16 = _____

2. $\frac{3}{5}$ of 45 = _____

3. $\frac{3}{4}$ of 36 = _____

4. $\frac{3}{4}$ of 12 = _____

5. $\frac{6}{8}$ of 80 = _____

6. $\frac{4}{5}$ of 60 = _____

⚠ Problems

Brain-teaser Simon draws 24 squares, six squares along and four squares down. He shades in $\frac{3}{8}$ of the squares. How many squares does Simon shade in?

_____

Brain-buster Nina counts out 36 pennies. She puts nine pennies in a row, and repeats this three more times. Nina then takes away $\frac{5}{6}$ of the pennies. How many pennies are left?

_____

Fractions of numbers

Fractions are numbers.
For example, $\frac{1}{2}$ of 10 is 5.

📋 Revise

To find a fraction of a number, divide by the denominator (bottom number).

$$\frac{1}{4} \text{ of } 12 = 12 \div 4 = 3$$

$$\frac{1}{3} \text{ of } 18 = 18 \div 3 = 6$$

$$\frac{1}{8} \text{ of } 16 = 16 \div 8 = 2$$

If the numerator (top number) of the fraction you are finding is not 1, first divide by the denominator, then multiply by the numerator.

$$\frac{1}{4} \text{ of } 12 = 3$$
↓
$$\text{so } \frac{3}{4} \text{ of } 12 = 3 \times 3 = 9$$

$$\frac{1}{3} \text{ of } 18 = 6$$
↓
$$\text{so } \frac{2}{3} \text{ of } 18 = 6 \times 2 = 12$$

$$\frac{1}{8} \text{ of } 16 = 2$$
↓
$$\text{so } \frac{5}{8} \text{ of } 16 = 2 \times 5 = 10$$

Getting mixed up? I can help!

Tips 💡

Divide the number by the denominator first, then multiply by the numerator if that is greater than 1.
Use your multiplication facts to help you.

🗨 Talk maths

Look at the problems below and talk them through aloud, explaining each step in the answer.

There are 30 books on the shelf. The children take $\frac{2}{5}$ of the books. How many books did they take?

First find $\frac{1}{5}$ ➡ 30 ÷ 5 = 6

Use your answer to find $\frac{2}{5}$ ➡ 6 × 2 = 12

The children took 12 books.

There are 32 children in a class. $\frac{7}{8}$ of the children bring a packed lunch. How many children is that?

32 ÷ 8 = 4   4 × 7 = 28

28 children take a packed lunch to school.

✔ Check

Answer these questions. Write number sentences to show how you solved them.

1. $\frac{1}{3}$ of 27 = _____

2. $\frac{2}{3}$ of 30 = _____

3. $\frac{6}{10}$ of 100 = _____

4. $\frac{3}{5}$ of 25 = _____

5. $\frac{5}{8}$ of 72 = _____

6. $\frac{9}{10}$ of 100 = _____

⚠ Problems

Brain-teaser Harry has £36 in the bank. He spends $\frac{3}{4}$ of his money. How much does Harry spend?

_____

Brain-buster There are 80 litres of petrol in the car tank. After a journey, $\frac{5}{8}$ of the petrol has been used. How many litres of petrol are left in the tank?

_____

Equivalent fractions

$\frac{1}{2}$ is equivalent to (or the same as) $\frac{2}{4}$.

Look at these two rectangles.

$\frac{1}{2}$ of one rectangle is the same as $\frac{2}{4}$ of the other rectangle.

$\frac{1}{2}$	$\frac{1}{2}$

$\frac{1}{4}$	$\frac{1}{4}$	$\frac{1}{4}$	$\frac{1}{4}$

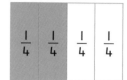

What other equivalent fractions can you see in the wall?

📋 Revise

This fraction wall shows how halves, quarters and eighths are related.

1							
$\frac{1}{2}$				$\frac{1}{2}$			
$\frac{1}{4}$		$\frac{1}{4}$		$\frac{1}{4}$		$\frac{1}{4}$	
$\frac{1}{8}$	$\frac{1}{8}$	$\frac{1}{8}$	$\frac{1}{8}$	$\frac{1}{8}$	$\frac{1}{8}$	$\frac{1}{8}$	$\frac{1}{8}$

Two $\frac{1}{2}$s are the same as one whole.

$\frac{1}{2}$ is equivalent to $\frac{2}{4}$ and $\frac{4}{8}$.

Here is a fraction wall for halves, fifths and tenths.

1									
$\frac{1}{2}$					$\frac{1}{2}$				
$\frac{1}{5}$		$\frac{1}{5}$		$\frac{1}{5}$		$\frac{1}{5}$		$\frac{1}{5}$	
$\frac{1}{10}$	$\frac{1}{10}$	$\frac{1}{10}$	$\frac{1}{10}$	$\frac{1}{10}$	$\frac{1}{10}$	$\frac{1}{10}$	$\frac{1}{10}$	$\frac{1}{10}$	$\frac{1}{10}$

$\frac{5}{10}$ are equivalent to $\frac{1}{2}$.

$\frac{2}{5}$ are equivalent to $\frac{4}{10}$.

Now look at this fraction wall for halves, thirds, sixths and ninths.

1								
$\frac{1}{2}$				$\frac{1}{2}$				
$\frac{1}{3}$			$\frac{1}{3}$			$\frac{1}{3}$		
$\frac{1}{6}$		$\frac{1}{6}$		$\frac{1}{6}$		$\frac{1}{6}$		$\frac{1}{6}$
$\frac{1}{9}$	$\frac{1}{9}$	$\frac{1}{9}$	$\frac{1}{9}$	$\frac{1}{9}$	$\frac{1}{9}$	$\frac{1}{9}$	$\frac{1}{9}$	$\frac{1}{9}$

$\frac{2}{6}$ are equivalent to $\frac{1}{3}$.

$\frac{3}{9}$ are also equivalent to $\frac{1}{3}$.

$\frac{1}{2}$ is equivalent to $\frac{3}{6}$.

Tips 💡

Look at the fraction walls above to help you see the fraction families.

💬 Talk maths

Here are some pairs of equivalent fractions.

$\frac{1}{3}$ and $\frac{2}{6}$ $\frac{3}{4}$ and $\frac{6}{8}$ $\frac{1}{3}$ and $\frac{3}{6}$ $\frac{3}{5}$ and $\frac{6}{10}$

$\frac{1}{4}$ and $\frac{2}{8}$ $\frac{2}{3}$ and $\frac{6}{9}$ $\frac{2}{5}$ and $\frac{4}{10}$ $\frac{4}{5}$ and $\frac{8}{10}$

What do you notice about the numbers in each pair?

Your 2- and 3-times tables might help.

✔ Check

Use the fraction walls to answer these questions.

1. How many sixths are equivalent to $\frac{1}{3}$? _____

2. How many tenths are equivalent to $\frac{1}{2}$? _____

3. How many quarters are equivalent to $\frac{6}{8}$? _____

4. How many ninths are equivalent to $\frac{2}{3}$? _____

5. How many sixths make a whole? _____

6. How many sixths are equivalent to $\frac{1}{2}$? _____

⚠ Problems

Brain-teaser Jamie cuts a pizza into eight equal slices. He takes half of the pizza to eat. Susie takes a quarter of the pizza. How many slices of the pizza are left?

_____

Brain-buster Tom decides to divide a flowerbed into ten equal sections. He plants $\frac{1}{5}$ of the sections with flowers. In half of the sections he puts flowerpots. In two sections he puts garden gnomes. What fraction of the garden is left?

_____

Comparing and ordering fractions

↻ Recap

Look at the denominator of the fraction first. This tells you the total number of parts.

The numerator, the top number, tells you how many of the parts are being used.

This bar of chocolate has been divided into 12 equal parts.

So $\frac{1}{4}$ of the chocolate is three pieces.

And $\frac{3}{4}$ of the chocolate is 3 × 3 or nine pieces.

📄 Revise

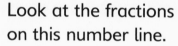

Where would $\frac{1}{6}$ go on the number line? What about $\frac{1}{8}$?

You can use a fraction number line to help you to compare and order fractions.

This number line shows eighths.

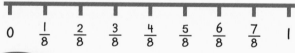

0   $\frac{1}{8}$ $\frac{2}{8}$ $\frac{3}{8}$ $\frac{4}{8}$ $\frac{5}{8}$ $\frac{6}{8}$ $\frac{7}{8}$ 1

Look at the numerators. What do you notice?

Look at the fractions on this number line.

0   $\frac{1}{5}$ $\frac{1}{4}$ $\frac{1}{3}$ $\frac{1}{2}$ 1

They are all unit fractions – the numerators are all 1. As the unit fractions get bigger, the denominator gets smaller.

Look at $\frac{1}{3}$ and $\frac{1}{2}$. Denominator 3 divides 1 into 3 parts. Denominator 2 divides 1 into 2 parts. So $\frac{1}{2}$ is larger than $\frac{1}{3}$.

💡 Tip

Use a fraction wall such as this to compare and order fractions.

$\frac{1}{2}$				$\frac{1}{2}$	
$\frac{1}{3}$		$\frac{1}{3}$		$\frac{1}{3}$	
$\frac{1}{4}$		$\frac{1}{4}$	$\frac{1}{4}$		$\frac{1}{4}$
$\frac{1}{6}$	$\frac{1}{6}$	$\frac{1}{6}$	$\frac{1}{6}$	$\frac{1}{6}$	$\frac{1}{6}$
$\frac{1}{8}$	$\frac{1}{8}$	$\frac{1}{8}$	$\frac{1}{8}$	$\frac{1}{8}$	$\frac{1}{8}$	$\frac{1}{8}$	$\frac{1}{8}$

💬 Talk maths

Compare $\frac{1}{3}$ and $\frac{1}{4}$ and find out which fraction is bigger.

Compare $\frac{1}{8}$ and $\frac{1}{10}$ and find out which fraction is the smallest.

How do you know?

> You can draw a fraction number line to help you.

✔ Check

1. **Order these fractions. Begin with the smallest.** $\frac{1}{2}, \frac{1}{6}, \frac{1}{5}, \frac{1}{3}$

   _____

2. **Order these fractions. Begin with the smallest.** $\frac{3}{8}, \frac{2}{8}, \frac{7}{8}, \frac{5}{8}$

   _____

3. **Put these fractions in order. Begin with the smallest.** $\frac{7}{10}, \frac{5}{10}, \frac{9}{10}, \frac{1}{10}$

   _____

⚠ Problems

Brain-teaser Sam cuts a cake. His little sister Emily asks him whether $\frac{1}{3}$ or $\frac{1}{2}$ of the cake would be bigger. What is the correct answer to tell Emily?

_____

Brain-buster Grandad offers Sam some pocket money. He can choose to have $\frac{1}{3}$ of £15 or $\frac{1}{5}$ of £20. Which offer gives Sam more pocket money?

_____

Adding and subtracting fractions with the same denominator

↻ Recap

All these fractions belong to the same family.
The fractions have 8 as their denominator.

$$\frac{1}{8} \qquad \frac{2}{8} \qquad \frac{3}{8} \qquad \frac{4}{8} \qquad \frac{5}{8} \qquad \frac{6}{8} \qquad \frac{7}{8} \qquad \frac{8}{8}$$

Revise

We can add and subtract fractions that have the same denominator.

You can use a fraction number line to count on or back.

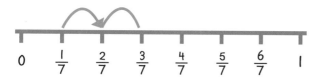

$$\frac{1}{7} + \frac{2}{7} = \frac{3}{7}$$

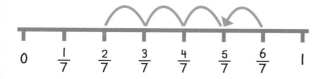

$$\frac{6}{7} - \frac{4}{7} = \frac{2}{7}$$

Or you can just add or subtract the numerators, or top numbers.

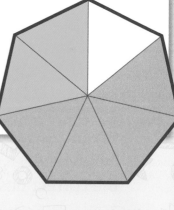

$$\frac{1}{7} + \frac{2}{7} = \frac{1 + 2}{7} = \frac{3}{7}$$

$$\frac{6}{7} - \frac{4}{7} = \frac{6 - 4}{7} = \frac{2}{7}$$

Remember, you only add the numerators.

When the numerator and denominator are the same, the fraction equals one.

Tips

Sometimes two fractions make a whole one.

$$\frac{3}{7} + \frac{4}{7} = \frac{3 + 4}{7} = \frac{7}{7} = 1$$

 Talk maths

Talk about pairs of fractions that equal one. Share at least two examples.

Talk about how you would solve these these sums. Would you use a number line or a different method? Explain why you say that.

$\frac{2}{8} + \frac{4}{8}$ $\frac{4}{8} - \frac{2}{8}$ $\frac{6}{9} + \frac{2}{9}$ $\frac{7}{9} - \frac{3}{9}$

✔ Check

Try to work mentally.

You can draw fraction number lines to help you if necessary.

1. $\frac{4}{8} + \frac{3}{8} =$ _____

2. $\frac{9}{10} - \frac{3}{10} =$ _____

3. $\frac{6}{7} - \frac{3}{7} =$ _____

4. $\frac{4}{6} + \frac{2}{6} =$ _____

5. $\frac{3}{5} - \frac{2}{5} =$ _____

6. $\frac{5}{6} - \frac{4}{6} =$ _____

⚠ Problems

Brain-teaser Rachel eats $\frac{5}{10}$ of a bar of chocolate and Lorna eats $\frac{4}{10}$. How much do they eat altogether? How much is left over?

_____

Brain-buster Jamie, Susie and Penny have a pizza cut into 12 slices. Jamie eats $\frac{6}{12}$ of the pizza. Susie eats $\frac{3}{12}$ of the pizza. How much is left for Penny to have?

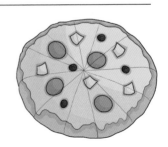

_____

Solving fraction problems

↺ Recap

A whole 1 can be written in different ways. For example,

$$1 \qquad \frac{4}{4} \qquad \frac{8}{8}$$

To add or subtract fractions, check the denominators are the same, then add or subtract the numerators.

📃 Revise

You can solve problems with fractions. Remember the strategies you used to solve problems with whole numbers.

Here is a missing number problem.

$$\frac{6}{8} - \bigstar = \frac{1}{8}$$

Decide what you need to work out. What number do you need to subtract from $\frac{6}{8}$ to get to $\frac{1}{8}$?

Count back in eighths from $\frac{6}{8}$ to $\frac{1}{8}$:

$\frac{5}{8}, \frac{4}{8}, \frac{3}{8}, \frac{2}{8}, \frac{1}{8}$ is five eighths.

$\frac{6}{8} - \frac{5}{8} = \frac{1}{8}$, so the missing number is $\frac{5}{8}$.

> You can draw a fraction number line to help you.

Or you can work out:

$$\frac{6}{8} - \frac{1}{8} = \frac{6-1}{8} = \frac{5}{8}$$

Here is a word problem.

> Freya eats $\frac{2}{5}$ of a bar of chocolate. How much of the chocolate is left?

You can write this as a missing number problem.

$$\frac{2}{5} + \bigstar = \frac{5}{5} \text{ or } 1$$

Decide what you need to work out. What number do you need to add to $\frac{2}{5}$ to get to 1?

Count on in fifths from $\frac{2}{5}$ to 1: $\frac{3}{5}, \frac{4}{5}, \frac{5}{5}$.

$\frac{2}{5} + \frac{3}{5} = 1$, so there is $\frac{3}{5}$ of the bar of chocolate left.

Or you can work out:

$$1 - \frac{2}{5} = \frac{5}{5} - \frac{2}{5} = \frac{5-2}{5} = \frac{3}{5}$$

💡 Tip

Read the question carefully, then write a number sentence.

When adding or subtracting fractions, make sure the denominators are the same.

 Talk maths

Look at the problems below and talk them through aloud.
Which method do you prefer?

$$\frac{3}{10} + \star = \frac{7}{10}$$

Count on: $\frac{4}{10}, \frac{5}{10}, \frac{6}{10}, \frac{7}{10}$

The missing number is $\frac{4}{10}$

Subtract: $\frac{7}{10} - \frac{3}{10} = \frac{7-3}{10} = \frac{4}{10}$

The missing number is $\frac{4}{10}$

There is $\frac{7}{8}$ of a chocolate cake left. Joe eats some of the cake. Now there is $\frac{5}{8}$ left. What fraction of the cake did Joe eat?

$\frac{7}{8} - \star = \frac{5}{8}$

Count back: $\frac{6}{8}, \frac{5}{8}$

Joe ate $\frac{2}{8}$ of the cake.

Subtract: $\frac{7}{8} - \frac{5}{8} = \frac{7-5}{8} = \frac{2}{8}$ → Joe ate $\frac{2}{8}$ of the cake.

✔ Check

1. Find the missing number.
   $\star + \frac{4}{7} = \frac{5}{7}$ _____

2. What is the difference between $\frac{2}{7}$ and $\frac{5}{7}$? _____

3. Find the missing number.
   $\star - \frac{3}{9} = \frac{2}{9}$ _____

4. What is the sum of $\frac{5}{12}$ and $\frac{4}{12}$? _____

⚠ Problems

Brain-buster There are 12 bottles of juice on the counter. The first customer buys $\frac{3}{12}$ of the juice. The second customer buys $\frac{5}{12}$ of the juice. What fraction of the bottles of juice is left?

_____

Measuring and comparing lengths

↻ Recap

To write lengths, we use these units of measurement:

metres (m)   centimetres (cm)   millimetres (mm)

When recording a length, always write the units of measurement.
You can use the shortened form of m, cm or mm.

1m = 100cm

📝 Revise

You will need a ruler that is marked in cm and mm.

To measure a line, place 0cm on your ruler pointing to the end of the line.

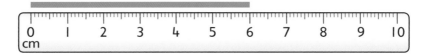

This line is 6cm long.

Before you measure a line, estimate how long you think it is. Compare your estimate and measurement to see how accurate you were.

This line is longer than 7cm and shorter than 8cm.

Find the mark on the ruler for $7\frac{1}{2}$cm or 7cm 5mm. This is halfway between 7cm and 8cm.

Count on in millimetres from there to where the line ends.

The line is 7.8cm long, or 7cm 8mm.

There are 10mm in 1cm.

Comparing lengths

We can compare two lines like this.

A 7cm 8mm line is shorter than a 9cm 3mm line.

7cm 8mm < 9cm 3mm

Or we could say that a 9cm 3mm line is longer than a 7cm 8mm line.

9cm 3mm > 7cm 8mm

🗨 *Talk maths*

Look at your pencil. How long do you think it is?

Now measure it carefully. Don't forget to count any millimetres too!
Did you make a reasonable estimate?

Now do the same for your book. Estimate its length first, then measure.

Now do the same for its width. Estimate then measure.

Now compare your estimates and measures.

Practise this with other things around you. You will find that your
estimates become more accurate.

✔ Check

1. **Draw these lines as accurately as you can.**

    a. $8\frac{1}{2}$cm

    b. 9cm 6mm

2. **Write the answers for these. Show your working out.**

a. What is the total length of two lines measuring 8cm 4mm and 9cm 5mm?

_____

b. How much longer is $7\frac{1}{2}$cm than 7cm 4mm? _____

⚠ Problems

Brain-teaser Mr Smith asks Paul to draw a line that is 10cm 4mm long. Paul
draws a line that is 9cm 8mm long. What is the difference in the two lengths?

_____

Brain-buster Jon has a 35m length of rope. He cuts off 17m. Then he cuts the
remaining piece of rope into two equal pieces. How long are each of the two
equal pieces of rope?

_____

Measuring and comparing mass

↺ Recap

Mass is measured in kilograms (kg) and grams (g).

1kg = 1000g

Revise

Look at the dial. It is measuring in hundreds.

Count around the dial in 0g, 100g, 200g...
and so on to 1000g.

1000g is the same as 1kg.

The arrow points to 300g. So the mass is 300g.

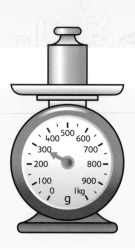

Now look at this dial.

This time the count is in 200s. 0g, 200g, 400g... to 1kg.

The arrow is midway between 600g and 800g, so the mass is 700g.

We can compare the two masses like this.

The 300g mass is lighter than the 700g mass.

300g < 700g

💡 Tip

Check the numbers on the dial.
Remember, the arrow may point in between two numbers.

Always write the units of measurement with your answer: kilograms or kg, grams or g.

Use my tips to help you read scales accurately!

💬 Talk maths

This dial counts up in 500s.

Read the labels on the scale aloud.

Can you say them in grams? 0g, 500g...

The arrow is pointing halfway between 500g and 1kg. So the mass is 750g.

Explain to a friend or adult how you could work that out.

Tell them what the reading halfway between 1kg and 1½kg would be.

What about the reading halfway between 1½kg and 2kg?

✔ Check

1. **Write the reading on each dial in grams.**

    a. _____

    b. _____

    c. _____

    d. _____

2. **Use < or > to show which is heavier, the mass of c or the mass of d.**

    c _____ d

a.  **b.**

c. 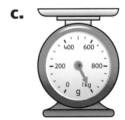 **d.**

⚠ Problems

Brain-teaser Martha is making bread. She needs 400g of flour. She pours the flour out onto the scale pan. The reading on the dial is 500g. How much flour does Martha need to take off the pan?

_____

Brain-buster Alfie weighs some tins. The first one weighs 340g, the second one weighs 350g and the third one weighs 330g. What is the difference in mass between the lightest and the heaviest tin?

_____

Measuring and comparing volume and capacity

↺ Recap

Volume and capacity are measured in litres (l) or millilitres (ml).

1 litre = 1000 millilitres

Revise

Here is a measuring jug.

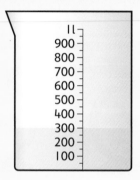

Look carefully at the scale.

The scale goes up in 100ml. 0, 100, 200, 300... and so on to 1 litre.

The capacity of the jug is 1 litre.

1 litre is the same as 1000ml.

The water level is at 300ml. So the volume of the water is 300ml.

Here is another measuring jug.

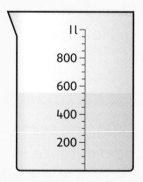

The water in the jug comes to halfway between 500ml and 600ml.

So the volume of the water is 550ml.

You can compare two amounts of water.

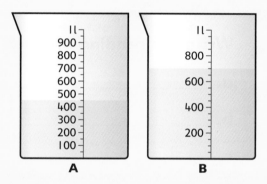

The water in jug A comes to halfway between 400ml and 500ml. This is 450ml.

The water in jug B comes to halfway between 600ml and 800ml. This is 700ml.

450ml < 700ml so there is more water in jug B.

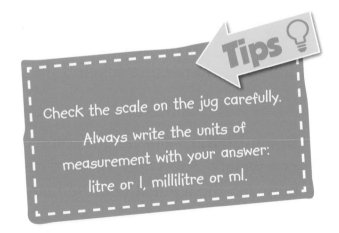

Tips

Check the scale on the jug carefully.

Always write the units of measurement with your answer: litre or l, millilitre or ml.

💬 Talk maths

Here are two measuring jugs.

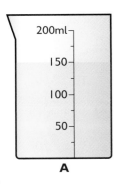 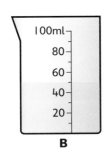

A   B

Jug A measures in 50ml. The scale goes 0ml, 50ml, 100ml, 150ml, 200ml.

Jug B measures in 20ml. The scale goes up in 20ml steps.

Which jug has more water in it?

If you used jug B to fill jug A, how many times would you need to fill it?

✔ Check

1. What is the capacity of the jug?
_____

2. What is the volume of the water in the jug?
_____

3. Another 200ml is poured into the jug. What is the volume of the water now?
_____

4. Next, 400ml is poured out of the jug. How much water is left in the jug?
_____

5. How much more water do you now need to fill the jug to the 1 litre mark?
_____

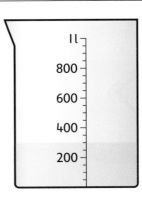

⚠ Problems

Brain-buster A Juicy Juice bottle contains 1 litre of juice. The glasses on the table each hold 300ml. How many glasses can be filled? How much juice is left in the bottle?

_____

Telling the time with analogue clocks

↻ Recap

There are 24 hours in a day.

Clock faces show 12 hours.

They are usually numbered 1 to 12.

There are 60 minutes in each hour.

On a clock, there are 5 minutes between each number.

Revise

Make sure you can tell the time to the nearest minute.

The minute hand is in the first half of the clock.

Count on from the 3 (15 minutes past) until you reach the minute hand: 16, 17, 18, 19.

The hour hand is just past the 7.

The clock shows 19 minutes past 7.

The minute hand is in the second half of the clock.

Count on anticlockwise from the 8 (20 minutes to) until you reach the minute hand: 21, 22, 23.

The hour hand is coming up to 11.

The clock shows 23 minutes to 11.

Tips 💡

Remember, if the minute hand is in the first 30 minutes, the time is 'past' the hour. If the minute hand is in the second 30 minutes, the time is 'to' the next hour.

For minutes past the hour, start at 12 and count in fives for each number on the clock until you reach the minute hand. Then count on in ones for any more minutes.

For minutes to the next hour, start at 12 and count anticlockwise in fives for each number on the clock until you reach the minute hand. Then count on in ones for any extra minutes.

Talk maths

What is your favourite time of day?

Draw the time on the clock.

Tell a friend or adult about your favourite time of day.

✔ Check

1. **Draw hands on the clock faces to show these times.**

a. 19 minutes past 7

b. 24 minutes to 8

c. 17 minutes to 1

2. **Write the time for these clocks.**

a. _____

b. _____

⚠ Problems

Brain-teaser Tim thinks the time is 24 minutes to five. Barry thinks the time is 24 minutes past four. The clock shows the minute hand at just past the 7. Who is telling the correct time?

_____

Brain-buster At the end of the lesson the time is a quarter to 11. Playtime lasts until five minutes past 11. How long is playtime?

_____

Telling the time with Roman numerals

↻ Recap

There are 24 hours in a day. Clock faces show 12 hours.

There are 60 minutes in each hour.

On a clock, there are 5 minutes between each number.

Revise

Clocks do not always have the numerals we use in maths.

This clock uses Roman numerals.

You can tell the time in the same way with these numerals.

Here are some Roman numerals.

I	V	X
1	5	10

All the other numerals on the clock are made from these.

I	II	III	IV	V	VI	VII	VIII	IX	X	XI	XII
1	2	3	4	5	6	7	8	9	10	11	12

Look at IV. This shows 1 less than 5.

VI shows 1 more than 5.

VII shows 2 more than 5.

VIII shows 3 more than 5.

IX shows 1 less than 10.

XI is 1 more than 10.

XII is 2 more than 10.

DID YOU KNOW?

A famous clock with Roman numerals is Big Ben.

Roman numerals are tricky, but my tips will help!

Tips 💡

Sometimes clocks with Roman numerals use IIII for IV. There's a simple rule with Roman numerals. Any I before V or X means the number is 1 less than 5 or 10. Any I after V means it is 1 more than 5. The same works with X.

💬 Talk maths

Do you have any clocks or watches with Roman numerals at home? See if you can find one and read the time on it.

Look at a church tower with a clock. Does that have ordinary numerals or Roman numerals? Read the time on any of these clocks that you see.

✔ Check

1. How many minutes past the hour?

2. How many minutes to the hour?

3. Draw in the hands to show these times on the clock faces below.

a. Quarter past 6

b. 27 minutes to 9

c. 27 minutes past 9

⚠ Problems

Brain-teaser Sam's watch has Roman numerals. The hour hand points to just past V and the minute hand points to II. What is the time?

Brain-buster The Roman numeral clock minute hand points to one minute past VI. The hour hand is past VIII. What is the time?

Telling the time with a 24-hour clock

↺ Recap

There are 24 hours in each day.
Midnight is 12 o'clock at night.
Noon is 12 o'clock in the day.

🗒 Revise

This clock shows the hours from midnight to noon, then the hours from noon to midnight.

Count around the clock:

1, 2, 3..., 12, 13, 14..., 22, 23, 0.

Digital clocks and watches usually tell the time using the 24-hour clock. On a digital clock:

- 02:30 means half past two in the morning
- 14:30 means half past two in the afternoon
- 00:15 means a quarter past midnight.

Subtract 12 from the 24-hour time to find the 12-hour time.

When we write times in digits, we count on for minutes past the hour, all the way to 59. So 15:34 means 34 minutes past 3 in the afternoon, or 26minutes to 4 in the afternoon.

For 12-hour time we use am and pm:

- 12:27am means 27 minutes past 12 in the morning (or past midnight).
- 12:27pm means 27 minutes past 12 in the afternoon.

💡 Tip

On an ordinary clock you cannot tell if the time is am or pm.
On a digital watch set to 24-hour clock time you can tell whether it is morning or afternoon.
am times start with the digits 00–11,
pm times start with the digits 12–23.
Remember to use 'am' or 'pm' when writing 12-hour times.

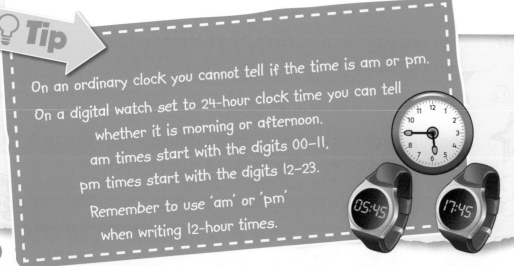

💬 Talk maths

Read the time on these clocks.

Are they am times, pm times, or can't you tell?

Make up a story about what you might be doing at these three times of day.

✔ Check

1. **Write these times in 24-hour clock time.**

a. Half past six in the morning

_____

b. 8:45pm

_____

c. 27 minutes to four in the afternoon

_____

d. 10 minutes to three in the afternoon

_____

e. 12:07am

_____

f. Quarter past four in the morning.

_____

⚠ Problems

Brain-teaser Khalid sets the alarm on his digital clock to ring at 23 minutes to seven in the morning. What time does the clock show when it rings?

_____

Brain-buster Peter reads the time on his Roman numeral clock as the hour hand points to beyond X and the minute hand to two minutes past VIII. It is evening. Write the time in 24-hour clock time.

_____

Using the vocabulary of time

↻ Recap

You use the vocabulary of time in everyday life.

Yesterday, I went to the library.

Revise

Here is some of the vocabulary of time that we use often in everyday life.

> morning   afternoon   noon   midnight   am   pm
>
> day   hour   minute   second

Here are some sentences that use some of these words.

Molly ran a race. She took 15 seconds to reach the finish line.

This morning it took me 2 minutes to really clean my teeth thoroughly.

The journey to London took 3 hours by train.

We can order these events by how long each one took.

15 seconds is the shortest time. 3 hours is the longest time.

So, 15 seconds < 2 minutes < 3 hours. This is from the shortest to the longest time.

And 3 hours > 2 minutes > 15 seconds. This is from the longest to the shortest time.

Some digital watches show time in hours, minutes and seconds like this one.

It shows an evening time.

The time is 8:15pm and 14 seconds.

Sometimes we need to calculate with time.

Timothy writes his name eight times in 72 seconds.

How long does he take to write his name once?

72 ÷ 8 = 9

So Timothy takes nine seconds to write his name once.

Tips

Always check the units of time that you are working with.

If you are timing an event, it may be in seconds, minutes or even hours.

🗨 Talk maths

Here are some sentences that use the vocabulary of time.
Read each one and look for words to do with time.

I get up in the morning at 7:30am.   I go to bed at 8:30pm.

I am sound asleep by midnight.   I have my school dinner at noon.

Now think of your own sentences about time. Try to use all the words in the box on the opposite page.

✔ Check

1. **Write the missing time word in these sentences.**

   a. In the _____ I have my breakfast at 8:00.

   b. I come home from school in the _____ at 4:00.

   c. At school we have our lunch at _____, which is when the afternoon starts.

2. **a.** Which takes longer, 35 seconds or half a minute?

   _____

   b. Which is the shorter time, one day or 23 hours and 59 minutes?

   _____

⚠ Problems

Brain-teaser Which is shorter, 1 minute and 15 seconds or 70 seconds?

_____

Brain-buster Georgiana writes her name six times. This takes her 48 seconds. How many seconds does it take her to write her name just once?

_____

Numbers and time

↻ Recap

There are seven days in a week:
Monday, Tuesday, Wednesday, Thursday,
Friday, Saturday and Sunday.

📝 Revise

You need to learn these time facts.

There are 60 seconds in one minute.

There are 60 minutes in one hour.

There are 24 hours in one day.

There are 365 days in one year.

In a leap year there are 366 days.

There is a leap year every fourth year.

A leap year number is exactly divisible by 4.

DID YOU KNOW?

There are 3600 seconds in an hour and 86,400 seconds in one day!

Use this poem to help you remember the number of days in the months of the year.

> Thirty days has September,
>
> April, June, and November.
>
> All the rest have 31,
>
> Except for February all alone,
>
> It has 28 each year,
>
> but 29 each leap year.

Tips

To work out if it is a leap year look at the last two numbers in the year. If it divides exactly by 4 it is a leap year. So, for 2016, look at just the 16. And 16 does divide by 4, so 2016 is a leap year.

Here are the months and their days set out in a table.

Jan	Feb	Mar	Apr	May	Jun	Jul	Aug	Sep	Oct	Nov	Dec
31	28 or 29	31	30	31	30	31	31	30	31	30	31

 Talk maths

Look at these problems and talk them through aloud. Explain each step in the answers.

How many days are there from 15th March to the end of the month (not including the 15th)?

There are 31 days in March.

31 − 15 = 16 days

Tom times himself doing his homework. He starts at 4:35pm and finishes at 5:12pm. How long does he take?

Count around the clock from 4:35.

35 to 40, 50, 60 is 25 minutes.

5:00 to 5:12 is 12 minutes.

25 + 12 = 37 minutes

So Tom's homework takes 37 minutes.

✔ Check

1. **Write your working as well as the answers for these questions.**

a. How long is it from 2nd December to the end of the month (not including the 2nd)? _____

b. How long is it from 6:30pm to 7:45pm? _____

c. How many minutes are there in 3 hours? _____

d. How long is 90 seconds in minutes and seconds? _____

⚠ Problems

Brain-teaser Janie runs to school in 6 minutes 15 seconds. Peter runs to school in 6 minutes 27 seconds. How much longer does Peter take than Janie?

_____

Brain-buster Kerry decides to make a cake. It takes her 6 minutes to find the ingredients, 2 minutes to weigh the ingredients and 10 minutes to mix the ingredients. The cake takes 35 minutes to bake. How many minutes is that in total? _____

Finding the perimeter of 2D shapes

↻ Recap

2D shapes include triangles, squares, rectangles, pentagons, hexagons and circles.

Revise

Perimeter is the distance all the way around a 2D shape.

The perimeter of this rectangle is

3cm + 2cm + 3cm + 2cm = 10cm

To find the permimeter we measure each side, then we add them together.

3cm

2cm   2cm

3cm

You can find the perimeter of any 2D shape in the same way.

1.5cm

1.5cm   1.5cm

1.5cm

The perimeter of the square is

1.5mm + 1.5mm + 1.5mm + 1.5mm = 6mm

The perimeter is the distance an ant would walk if it went all the way around the shape.

This time there are six sides to add.

Here is an irregular hexagon.

The perimeter of the hexagon is

16m + 16m + 5m + 5m + 5m + 5m
= 32m + 20m
= 52m

5m

16m   5m

   5m

16m   5m

💡 Tip

Make sure the units of all the lengths are the same before you add.

You can add centimetres to centimetres, metres to metres and millimetres to millimetres.

Trace around the shape with your finger to make sure you include all the sides.

 Talk maths

Explain to a friend or adult how to find the perimeter of these shapes.

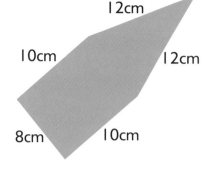

- The green shape.

- All four sides of a square measure 7cm. Find the perimeter.

- A triangle has two sides that measure 6cm each and one side that measures 10cm. Find the perimeter.

✔ Check

1. **Measure and find the perimeters of these shapes.**

a.

b.

c.

_____   _____   _____

2. **Find the perimeters of these shapes.**

a. A garden with six sides all 10m in length. _____

b. A triangle with sides measuring 7cm, 8cm and 13cm. _____

⚠ Problems

Brain-teaser Riley cuts out a regular hexagon from paper. Each side of the hexagon measures 8cm. What is the perimeter of the hexagon?

_____

Brain-buster A computer tablet is a rectangle shape. It is 19cm along its width and 25cm in length. What is its perimeter?

_____

Money

↻ Recap

Here are our coins.

We also have £5, £10, £20 and £50 notes.

100p = £1

📝 Revise

If you are given an amount in pence, you can write it in pounds and pence by seeing how many lots of 100p there are. For example,

546p = 500p + 46p   500p = £5

So 546p is £5 and 46p. We write this as £5.46.

> Can you count on from 87p to £1 in your head?

You can find the difference between amounts of money by counting up. This is useful for finding change. For example, Polly buys a comic for 87p and pays with a £1 coin. Count on from 87p to £1 to find her change.

87p   90p   £1

Change = 3p + 10p = 13p

Or you can write a subtraction sentence: £1 − 87p = 100p − 87p = 13p

Here is one way of working out £3.45 plus £2.67.

£3.45 = 345p ,   £2.67 = 267p

	3	4	5
+	2	6	7
		1	2
	1	0	0
	5	0	0
	6	1	2

612p = £6.12

> **Tips** 💡
>
> To find the sum of several amounts of money, change them all to pence first then add them together. Change them back to pounds and pence at the end.

💬 Talk maths

Look at the problems below and talk them through aloud. Do you prefer to count on using a number line, or in your head? Why?

£4.50

I have £5. I want to buy this DVD.

How much change will I get?

| +10p | +10p | +10p | +10p | +10p |

£4 and 50p   £4 and 60p   £4 and 70p   £4 and 80p   £4 and 90p   £5

Count on: £4 and 50p, then 60, 70, 80, 90, £5
That is a count of 50p. The change is 50p.

> Talk about buying different items with different prices.

✔ Check

1. Show your working out.

a. Find 65p + 47p. Answer in £ and p.

b. Find £1 − 38p.

_____

c. Find the sum of £3.32 and £4.89.

d. How much more is £2.34 than £1.67?

_____

⚠ Problems

Brain-teaser Shani buys a drink of squash for 85p. How much change does she get from £5?

_____

Brain-buster Dan spends 75p on a drink, 37p on a biscuit and 46p on an apple. How much change does Dan get from £5?

_____

Adding and subtracting lengths

Lengths are measured in metres (m), centimetres (cm) and millimetres (mm).

1m = 100cm   1cm = 10mm

Revise

When working with lengths, always check the units of measurement. Add or subtract the same units.

To find the total of 3m 30cm and 2m 80cm, change the metres to centimetres.

330cm + 280cm

$$= 300 + 30 + 200 + 80$$
$$= 300 + 200 + 30 + 80$$
$$= 500 + 110$$
$$= 610cm \text{ or } 6m \text{ } 10cm$$

💡 Tip

Remember that 10mm is the same as 1cm.

And 100cm is the same as 1m.

When you add or subtract lengths, make sure the units of measurement are the same.

To find the difference between two lengths, subtract the shorter length from the longer.

My pencil used to be 19cm long. Now it is 15cm long.

How much of my pencil has gone?

We must find the difference between 19cm and 15cm.

19cm − 15cm is 4cm, so the pencil is 4cm shorter than it used to be.

This subtraction problem has mixed units.

Work out 5m 60cm − 3m 46cm.

First change the units to centimetres.

5m 60cm is 560cm and 3m 46cm is 346cm.

Here is one way of doing the subtraction.

	5	$^5\cancel{6}$	$^1 0$
−	3	4	6
	2	1	4

The answer is 214cm or 2m 14cm.

💬 Talk maths

Look at the problem below and talk it through aloud. Which method do you prefer?

> What is 15cm 9mm add 24cm 7mm?

Convert both lengths to millimetres first.

15cm 9mm = 159mm

24cm 7mm = 247mm

	1	5	9
+	2	4	7
	4	0	6
		1	1

15cm 9mm + 24cm 7mm

= 406mm or 40cm 6mm

Or add the centimetres and millimetres separately.

15cm + 24cm = 39cm

9mm + 7mm = 16mm

Convert the millimetres length to centimetres and millimetres.

16mm = 1cm 6mm

Then add it to 39cm.

39cm + 1cm 6mm = 40cm 6mm.

✔ Check

1. Find the answers. Use a separate piece of paper for working out.

a. Work out 64cm − 35cm.

b. Work out 156m + 247m.

c. Find the sum of 6cm 2mm and 3cm 9mm.

d. What is the difference between 2cm 4mm and 5cm 6mm?

⚠ Problems

Brain-teaser Freddie's mum measures him each birthday. When he was seven his height was 1 metre 25 centimetres. When he was eight he was 1 metre 33 centimetres. How much has he grown in one year?

Adding and subtracting mass

↻ Recap

To find the difference between two masses, subtract the smaller mass from the larger one.

Mass is measured in kilograms (kg) and grams (g).

$$1kg = 1000g$$

📝 Revise

To find the difference between two masses, subtract the smaller mass from the larger one.

1kg is the same as 1000g.

So $\frac{1}{2}$kg is 500g,

$\frac{1}{4}$kg is 250g and

$\frac{3}{4}$kg is 750g.

Use your favourite method to add masses in grams.

Here is one way of working out the total mass of these fruits

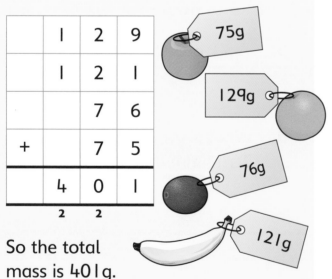

	1	2	9
	1	2	1
		7	6
+		7	5
	4	0	1
	2	2	

So the total mass is 401g.

Here is one way of working out the difference in mass between the heaviest and lightest of the four fruits above.

The orange is heaviest at 129g.

The apple is lightest at 75g.

Count on from 75 to 129: 75 to 100 is 25, and 100 to 129 is 29.

25 + 29 is 54.

So the difference in mass between the orange and apple is 54g.

Tips 💡

Be sure to show your working. This helps others to follow your thinking. You can draw a number line to help you to add or subtract masses.

🗨 *Talk maths*

Look at the scales below. Explain to a friend or adult which mass is smaller, then write a sentence to compare the two masses.

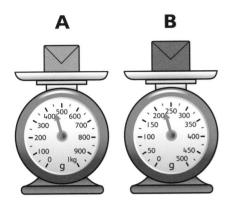

A   **B**

Can you complete this sentence?

_____ is the smaller mass.

Explain the method you would use to total the two masses and find the difference between the two masses.

✔ Check

1.   Find the answers. Use a separate piece of paper for working out.

a. 95g + 45g _____

b. 136g − 97g _____

c. 74g − 58g _____

d. What is the difference between 120g and 167g? _____

⚠ Problems

Brain-teaser Two children are going on a helicopter ride and have to be weighed beforehand. One child weighs 59kg. The other child weighs 52kg. How much is that in total? _____

Brain-buster Sara mixes together 100g of flour, 100g of sugar and 100g of butter. Then she adds three eggs, each of which weighs 56g. How much do the ingredients weigh in total?

_____

Adding and subtracting volume and capacity

↺ Recap

Capacity and volume are measured in litres (l) and millilitres (ml).

> 1 litre = 1000ml

📋 Revise

1 litre is the same as 1000ml.

So $\frac{1}{2}$ litre is 500ml,

$\frac{1}{4}$ litre is 250ml and

$\frac{3}{4}$ litre is 750ml.

Use your favourite methods to add and subtract volumes.

Tips 💡

Be sure to show your working. This helps others to follow your thinking. You can draw a number line to help you to add or subtract millilitres or litres.

Read the scale on this jug carefully.

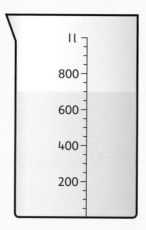

Capacity is how much a container can hold. This measuring jug has a capacity of 1000ml. It has a volume of 700ml in it.

It contains 700ml of water.

Another 200ml of water is added to the jug.

Add 200ml to 700ml to find the new volume of water.

700ml + 200ml = 900ml

450ml is poured away.

Subtract 450ml from 900ml to find the new volume of water.

900ml − 450ml = 450ml

Talk maths

Look at this problem and talk it through aloud with friend or adult.

There is 1 litre or 1000 millilitres of water in the jug.

450ml is poured out. How much is left in the jug?

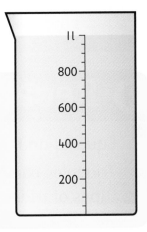

Use a number line to work out 1000ml − 450ml.

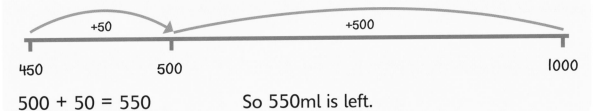

500 + 50 = 550   So 550ml is left.

✔ Check

1. **Answer these questions. Show your working out on a separate piece of paper.**

a. 65ml + 92ml _____

b. 135ml − 45ml _____

c. What is the sum of 230ml and 330ml? _____

d. What is the difference between 950ml and 760ml? _____

⚠ Problems

Brain-teaser A car has 80 litres of fuel in the tank at the start of a journey. At the end of the journey there is 32 litres of fuel left. How much fuel was used?

_____

Brain-buster A full litre jug is used to fill three 125ml cups. How much water is left in the jug?

_____

Lines

Squares and rectangles have four right angles. Triangles can have one right angle but most types of triangle have no right angles.

▤ Revise

Here is some vocabulary for lines.

> Perpendicular lines meet at a right angle.

| Horizontal | Vertical | Perpendicular | Parallel |

Look at this shape.

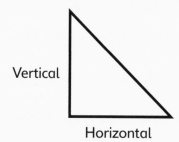

Vertical

Horizontal

It has one vertical line and one horizontal line.

The vertical and horizontal lines make a right-angle. They are perpendicular.

The shape is a right-angled triangle.

Here's another shape.

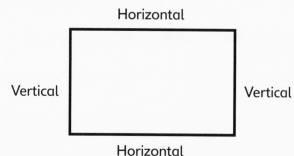

Horizontal

Vertical   Vertical

Horizontal

It has two vertical lines. They are parallel.

It has two horizontal lines. They are also parallel.

The vertical and horizontal lines are perpendicular. They make four right angles.

The shape is a rectangle.

Horizontal lines go across the page – like the **horizon**.
Vertical lines go up – people with **vertigo** don't like going up high.
Parallel lines run alongside each other – like train tracks.
Perpendicular lines make a right angle.

💬 Talk maths

Read this description aloud. Draw what you read.

This shape has three sides. One side is horizontal. One side is vertical. You should have drawn a scalene triangle.

Draw shapes. Describe them to a friend of adult (without showing them).

Use some of these words: horizontal, vertical, parallel, perpendicular.

Do their drawings match yours?

✔ Check

1. Are these lines parallel or perpendicular? _____

   a.

   b.

_____ _____

2. Draw a vertical line.

3. Draw a horizontal line.

4. Look at this shape.

   a. Label the horizontal lines **H**. Label the vertical lines **V**.

   b. Are any of the lines perpendicular? Write **P** where they meet.

   c. How many pairs of parallel lines does it have?

   _____

⚠ Problems

Brain-buster Beth draws a shape with eight sides. The opposite sides are parallel to each other and all the sides are the same length. What does she draw?

_____

Drawing 2D shapes

↻ Recap

Look back at page 76 to remind yourself what these words mean.

Some shapes have special lines.

These can be parallel, horizontal, vertical or perpendicular.

📋 Revise

To draw 2D shapes, you will need squared paper, a pencil, a ruler and a set square.

Follow these steps to draw a rectangle with sides of 8cm and 4cm.

1. First use a set square to draw a right angle.

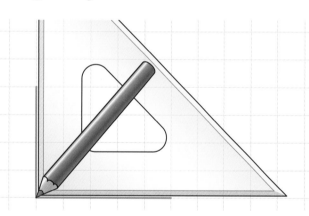

2. Then use a ruler to measure the length of the lines accurately.

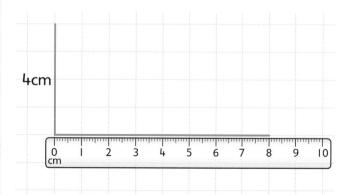

3. Use the set square to draw a second right angle.

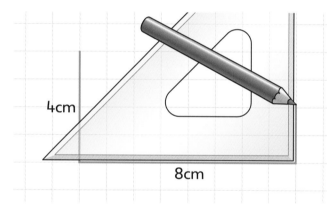

- Use a ruler to measure the length of the line accurately.

- Then join the top two corners to make a rectangle.

4. Use your set square to check the top two corners are right angles.

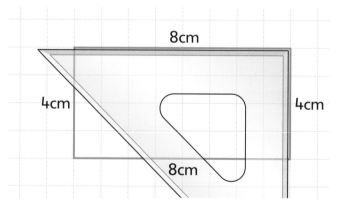

Talk maths

Try drawing some other shapes accurately.

Follow the steps on page 78 to draw a rectangle measuring 7cm by 6cm. Explain to a friend or adult what you are doing.

✔ Check

1. **Draw these shapes on squared paper.**

    a. A square with sides 7cm.

    b. A rectangle with sides 6cm and 10cm.

    c. An irregular pentagon. It must have one right angle and one side of 5cm.

    d. A right-angled triangle. The two perpendicular lines must be 6cm long.

⚠ Problems

Brain-teaser On a separate piece of paper. Draw a shape with four sides each 5cm and four right angles. Use a set square and ruler.
What shape have you drawn?

_____

Brain-buster A shape has four right angles and four sides, measuring 6cm, 6cm, 8cm and 8cm. The shape has two pairs of parallel sides.
What is the shape?

_____

Use a set square and ruler to draw the shape.

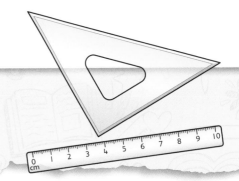

3D shapes

3D shapes are solid.

3D shapes have faces that are 2D shapes.

A vertex is where straight edges on a shape come together.

More than one vertex are called vertices.

> Look at the pictures of the shapes (or make them using modelling clay) and count the faces, vertices and edges. Did you count them all?

📋 Revise

Make sure you can name all of these 3D shapes.

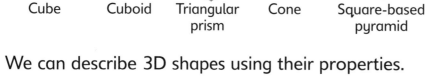

| Cube | Cuboid | Triangular prism | Cone | Square-based pyramid | Sphere |

We can describe 3D shapes using their properties.

The faces of these shapes are all flat.

3D shape	Number of faces	Number of vertices	Number of edges
Cube	6	8	12
Cuboid	6	8	12
Triangular prism	5	6	9
Square-based pyramid	5	5	8

These shapes have curves.

3D shape	Number of faces	Number of vertices	Number of edges
Cone	2	0	1
Sphere	1	0	0

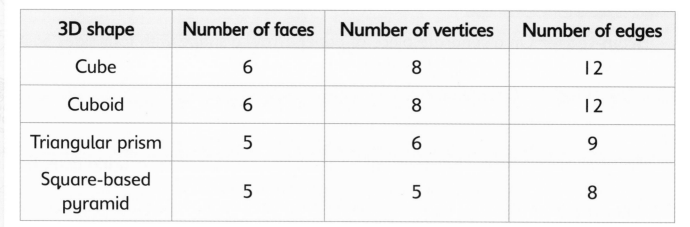

💬 Talk maths

Read this description of a 3D solid. What is it?

> I have six square faces.
>
> I have 12 vertices.
>
> I have eight edges.
>
> What am I?

Did you need all the clues, or was the first one enough?

Describe a different 3D solid to a friend of adult.

How many clues do you need to give them before they can guess what it is?

✔ Check

Cover up the charts on the opposite page with a piece of paper. Answer these questions using your memory.

1. **Name these shapes.**

a.

b.

c.

_____   _____   _____

2. **How many vertices does a triangular prism have?** _____

3. **How many faces does a square-based pyramid have?** _____

⚠ Problems

Brain-teaser I have four triangular faces. These come to a vertex. My base is square-shaped. What am I?

_____

Angles

↻ Recap

The point where two lines meet is called a vertex.

The space between the two lines is the angle.

The angle shows how much one line has turned on its vertex from the other.

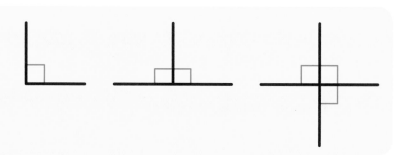

vertex

angle

📄 Revise

A right angle is a quarter turn.

Two right angles make a straight line, or a half turn.

Three right angles make three quarters of a turn.

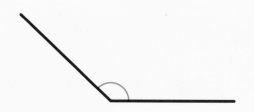

An acute angle is less than a right angle.

An obtuse angle is more than a right angle and less than two right angles.

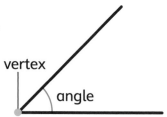

Don't get in a tangle with angles! Here are some tips to help you.

💡 Tip

Practise recognising angles. Look at some 2D shapes and decide what sort of angles they have.

The corner of a piece of paper is (usually!) a right angle. You can use this to check whether an angle is smaller (acute) or larger (obtuse) than a right angle.

💬 Talk maths

Ask a friend or adult to read these instructions aloud for you to follow.

Stand up.

Turn a quarter turn to the right.

You have turned through one right angle.

Now turn another quarter turn to the right.

You have turned through two right angles.

Turn again to the right for a quarter turn.

That is three-quarters of a full turn and is three right angles in total.

Turn once more a quarter turn to the right.

That is a full turn now. You have turned through four right angles.

✔ Check

1. **Name these angles. Are they acute, obtuse or right angles?**

a.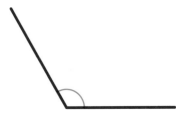

b.

c.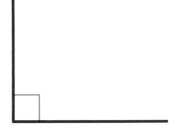

_____   _____   _____

2. **How many right angles make**

a. a half turn? _____   **b.** three quarters of a turn? _____

⚠ Problems

Brain-teaser Here is a 2D shape. Label each angle with the correct letter.
A = acute   O = obtuse   R = right angle
How many right angles are there?

_____

Tables and pictograms

↺ Recap

In a pictogram, each picture represents one or more items.

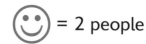 = 2 people

▤ Revise

Look at this pictogram.

Dogs entered for a local dog show   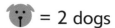 = 2 dogs

Irish setter	🐶🐶🐶🐶🐶🐶🐶
Labrador	🐶🐶🐶🐶🐶🐶🐶🐶🐶🐶🐶
Boxer	🐶🐶🐶🐶🐶🐶🐶🐶
Great Dane	🐶🐶
Border collie	🐶🐶🐶🐶🐶🐶🐶🐶🐶🐶🐶🐶
Corgi	🐶🐶🐶🐶🐶🐶
Bloodhound	🐶🐶🐶

- The title tells you what the data is about.
- This pictogram shows the number of dogs of different breeds that were entered in a local dog show.
- Look at the key. This tells you that one picture represents two dogs.
- Count in 2s to find the number of each breed of dog.

Look at the pictures for Irish setter.

There are 2, 4, 6, 8, 10, 12, 14 and then a half picture.

Half a picture represents one dog.

So there are 15 Irish setters.

Tips 💡

If you are asked to collect your own data use tallies. Count the tallies when you have collected all the data.

When making a pictogram make sure that the pictures are spaced evenly so that they can be compared easily across the pictogram.

Always read the key so you know what each picture represents.

💬 Talk maths

Look at these questions about the pictogram shown on the page opposite. Explain the answers to a friend or adult.

Which breed of dogs has the least number entered?

How many more Irish setters are there than corgis?

Make up some questions of your own about the pictogram.

If you get stuck, look at the key again.

✔ Check

The table shows the number of cats of different breeds that were entered in a local cat show.

1. Use the data to make a pictogram. Give it a title. Choose a picture to represent two cats.

Then answer the questions.

Cat breed	Numbers
Siamese	15
Ragdoll	18
Russian blue	11
British shorthair	20
Persian	13
Munchkin	10

a. How many cats are there if you total the munchkin, Russian Blue and British shorthair cats?

_____

b. Which breed has the least number of cats?

_____

Siamese							
Ragdoll							
Russian blue							
British shorthair							
Persian							
Munchkin							

c. Which breed has the greatest number of cats?

_____

⚠ Problems

Brain-teaser How many more Siamese need to be entered so that there is the same number as the British shorthair cats?

_____

Tables and bar charts

Bar charts are made in a similar way to pictograms, except the individual pictures become blocks.

🗒 Revise

Look at the scale on the bar chart. Each marker represents 2°C.

The temperature in February is 16°C.

The top of the bar for January is just below 16, so the temperature in January is 15°C.

The top of the bar for April is halfway between 20 and 24, so the temperature in April is 22°C.

This bar chart shows the average temperature each month in Orlando, USA

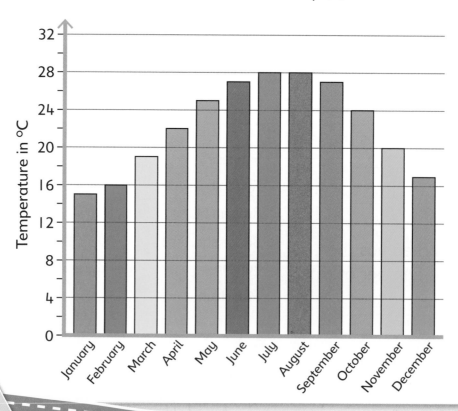

💡 **Tip**

Use squared paper when making bar charts. This helps you to be accurate in the size of the bar.

86

💬 Talk maths

Look at these questions about the bar chart on the opposite page.

Explain the answers to a friend or adult.

● Which are the hottest months?

● What is the difference in temperature between January and July?

✔ Check

The table shows the average sea temperatures each month in Orlando.

Jan	23°C	Jul	29°C
Feb	23°C	Aug	29°C
Mar	23°C	Sep	29°C
Apr	25°C	Oct	27°C
May	26°C	Nov	26°C
Jun	28°C	Dec	24°C

1. **Draw a bar chart for these temperatures. Give it a title. Then answer the questions.**

a. What is the sea temperature in October?

_____

b. By how much does the sea temperature rise between March and April?

_____

c. What is the difference between the hottest sea temperature and the coolest sea temperature?

_____

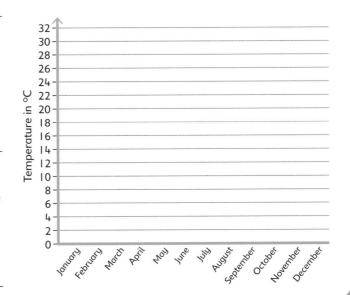

⚠ Problems

Brain-buster Look at both bar charts. Jamie loves swimming. He doesn't like the sea temperature to be above 25°C. He likes the land temperature to be at least 20°C. In which month would you suggest he goes to Orlando?

_____

Answers: Year 3

NUMBER AND PLACE VALUE

Page 9

1. 16, 24, 28, 32
2. 32, 40, 48, 64
3. 300, 350, 400
4. 500, 600, 700, 800
5. 700, 600, 500, 400

Brain-teaser: 0, 50, 100, 150, 200, 250, 300, 350, 400, 450, 500, 550, 600
Brain-buster: 16, 24, 32, 40, 48

Page 11

1. **a.** 365 **b.** 215
2. **a.** eight hundred and four **b.** nine hundred and seventy
3. 357, 537, 573, 735, 753
4. 321 > 243, 645 < 654, 720 > 702

Brain-buster: 245, 425, 524, 542

Page 13

1. 567
2. 576
3. 856
4. 300 + 70 + 9

Brain-teaser: 436
Brain-buster: 425

Page 15

1. 533
2. 591
3. 850
4. 432
5. 326
6. 49

Brain-teaser: £393
Brain-buster: £397

Page 17

1. **a.** 125, 165, 205 **b.** 300, 350, 400 **c.** 57, 47, 37
2. **a.** 11, 14, 17, **20**, 23, 26, 29 **b.** 96, 90, 84, **78**, **72**, **66**

Brain-teaser: 46, 49, 52, 55, 58, 61, 64
Brain-buster: 24, 34, 44, 54, 64, 74

Page 19

1. 659 – 100 = 559cm or 5m 59cm
2. 650 – 100 = 550, 550 + 10 = 560 litres
3. 180 + 10 = 190 seconds

Brain-teaser: 550
Brain-buster: 975

CALCULATIONS

Page 21

1. 397
2. 739
3. 431
4. 543
5. 521
6. 354

Brain-teaser: £702
Brain-buster: £159

Page 23

1. 103
2. 182
3. 727

Brain-teaser: **204**
Brain-buster: **751**

Page 25

1. 53
2. 178
3. 188

Brain-teaser: 368
Brain-buster: 303

Page 27

1. 95
2. 48
3. 690
4. 67
5. 403
6. 379

Brain-teaser: **257 metres**
Brain-buster: 306

Page 29

1. 71
2. 111
3. 34
4. 138
5. 95

Brain-teaser: £33
Brain-buster: £132

Page 31

1	72
2	11
3	12
4	27
5	12
6	48

Brain-teaser: **6**
Brain-buster: **8**

Page 33

1	69
2	17
3	32
4	24
5	92

Brain-teaser: **22cm**
Brain-buster: **7p**

Page 35

1	13
2	60
3	15
4	4
5	78

Brain-buster: **64 cartons juice and 128 snack packs**

FRACTIONS

Page 37

1	3
2	50
3	40
4	18
5	18
6	12

Brain-teaser: **21**
Brain-buster: **12 litres**

Page 39

1	2
2	27
3	27
4	9
5	60
6	48

Brain-teaser: **9**
Brain-buster: **6**

Page 41

1	9
2	20
3	60
4	15
5	45
6	90

Brain-teaser: **£27**
Brain-buster: **30 litres**

Page 43

1	2
2	5
3	3
4	6
5	6
6	3

Brain-teaser: **2**
Brain-buster: $\frac{1}{10}$

Page 45

1   $\frac{1}{6}, \frac{1}{5}, \frac{1}{3}, \frac{1}{2}$
2   $\frac{2}{8}, \frac{3}{8}, \frac{5}{8}, \frac{7}{8}$
3   $\frac{1}{10}, \frac{5}{10}, \frac{7}{10}, \frac{9}{10}$

Brain-teaser: $\frac{1}{2}$
Brain-buster: $\frac{1}{3}$ of £15

Page 47

1   $\frac{7}{8}$
2   $\frac{6}{10}$
3   $\frac{3}{7}$
4   1 or $\frac{6}{6}$
5   $\frac{1}{5}$
6   $\frac{1}{6}$

Brain-teaser: $\frac{9}{10}, \frac{1}{10}$
Brain-buster: $\frac{3}{12}$

Page 49

1   $\frac{1}{7}$
2   $\frac{3}{7}$
3   $\frac{5}{9}$
4   $\frac{9}{12}$

Brain-buster: $\frac{4}{12}$ or $\frac{1}{3}$

MEASUREMENT

Page 51

1   **a.** 8.5cm line drawn   **b.** 9.6cm line drawn

2   **a.** 17cm 9mm   **b.** 1mm

Brain-teaser: **6mm**
Brain-buster: **9m**

Page 53

1   **a.** 600g   **b.** 100g   **c.** 1000g   **d.** 750g

2   c > d

Brain-teaser: **100g**
Brain-buster: **20g**

Page 55

1   1 litre or 1l

2   300ml

3   500ml

4   100ml

5   900ml

Brain-buster: Three glasses, 100ml left in the bottle

Page 57

1   **a.** Hands set at 19 minutes past 7.
   b. Hands set at 24 minutes to 8.
   c. Hands set at 17 minutes to 1.

2   **a.** 11 minutes past 8. **b.** 28 minutes to 10.

Brain-teaser: Tim
Brain-buster: 20 minutes

Page 59

1   20

2   25

3   **a.** Hands set at a quarter past 6 **b.** Hands set at 27 minutes to 9
   c. Hands set at 27 minutes past 9

Brain-teaser: 10 minutes past 5
Brain-buster: 29 minutes to 9

Page 61

1   **a.** 06:30 **b.** 20:45 **c.** 15:33 **d.** 14:50 **e.** 00:07 **f.** 04:15

Brain-teaser: 06:37
Brain-buster: 22:42

Page 63

1   **a.** morning **b.** afternoon **c.** noon

2   **a.** 35 seconds **b.** 23 hours and 59 minutes

Brain-teaser: 70 seconds
Brain-buster: 8 seconds

Page 65

1   **a.** 29 days **b.** 1 hour 15 minutes **c.** 180 minutes
   d. 1 minute 30 seconds

Brain-teaser: 12 seconds
Brain-buster: 53 minutes

Page 67

1   **a.** 8cm **b.** 5cm **c.** 11cm

2   **a.** 60m **b.** 28cm

Brain-teaser: 48cm
Brain-buster: 88cm

Page 69

1   **a.** £1.12 **b.** 62p **c.** £8.21 **d.** 67p

Brain-teaser: £4.15
Brain-buster: £3.42

Page 71

1   **a.** 29cm **b.** 403m **c.** 10cm 1mm **d.** 3cm 2mm

Brain-teaser: 8cm

Page 73

1   **a.** 140g **b.** 39g **c.** 16g **d.** 47g

Brain-teaser: 111kg
Brain-buster: 468g

Page 75

1   **a.** 157ml **b.** 90ml **c.** 560ml **d.** 190ml

Brain-teaser: 48 litres
Brain-buster: 625ml

GEOMETRY

Page 77

1   **a.** Perpendicular **b.** Parallel

2   Vertical line drawn

3   Horizontal line drawn

4   **a.** One horizontal line labelled 'H', two vertical lines labelled 'V'

   b. 'P' written in two right angles **c.** One

Brain-buster: Regular octagon

Page 79

1   **a.** Square with sides of 7cm drawn. **b.** Rectangle with sides of 6cm and 10cm drawn. **c.** Irregular pentagon drawn. Check that it has an accurately drawn right angle, and that one side measures 5cm. **d.** Right-angled triangle with two sides of 6cm drawn.

Brain-teaser: Square with sides of 5cm drawn. Square.
Brain-buster: Rectangle. Rectangle with sides of 6cm and 8cm drawn.

Page 81

1   **a.** cube **b.** square-based pyramid **c.** cone

2   6

3   5

Brain-teaser: Pyramid

Page 82

1   **a.** obtuse angle **b.** acute angle **c.** right angle

2   **a.** 2 **b.** 3

Brain-teaser: One acute angle labelled 'A', one obtuse angle labelled 'O', two right angles labelled 'R'.

STATISTICS

Page 85

1   **a.** 41 **b.** Munchkin **c.** British shorthair

Brain-teaser: 5

Page 87

1   **a.** 27°C **b.** 2°C **c.** 6°C

Brain-buster: April

Glossary

< Less than
24 < 25 means 24 is less than 25.

> Greater than
25> 24 means 25 is greater than 24

A

Acute angle An angle that is less than a right angle.

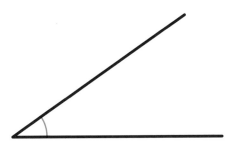

Analogue clock Shows the time with hands on a dial. The dial is numbered from 1 to 12 to mark 12 hours.

Ante meridian Before noon. Usually shortened to am.

B

Bar chart A bar chart has a bar for each item. The height of the bar represents how many there are. A bar chart is usually scaled, for example, one square represents five items.

C

Chunking This is a method of dividing. See example on page 32.

D

Denominator The number on the bottom of a fraction, which tells how many equal parts there are in total. In $\frac{2}{5}$ there are 5 equal parts.

Difference The amount between two numbers or measurements. For example the difference between 13 and 15 is 2.

Digit A single numeral such as 1, 5...9

Double Multiply a number by 2. Double 4 is 8.

E

Edge An edge is where two faces of a solid shape meet. At either end of an edge there will be a vertex.

Equivalent fractions Fractions with different numerators and denominators that are worth the same, such as $\frac{1}{2}$ and $\frac{2}{4}$.

Estimate A good guess of the answer. This usually involves some thought and a simplified calculation.

F

Face A flat or curved surface on a 3D shape.

Fraction A fraction is a part of a number, shape or measure that has been divided equally. For example, when a cake is cut into four equal slices, then one slice is $\frac{1}{4}$ of the cake.

H

Horizontal A horizontal line goes across the page.

I

Inverse Addition is the inverse of subtraction, and subtraction is the inverse of addition. 46 + 54 = 100, 100 − 46 = 54.

M

Mental methods Approaches for accurately solving calculations without writing them down

Multiplication is the inverse of division, and division is the inverse of multiplication. 6 × 5 = 30, 30 ÷ 5 = 6.

N

Numerator The top number of a fraction, which tells how many of the equal parts there are. In $\frac{2}{5}$. there are 2 equal parts out of 5.

O

Obtuse angle An angle that is greater than a right angle but less than two right angles.

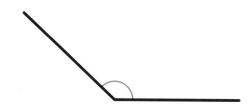

P

Parallel Parallel lines are always the same distance apart.

Partition Separate a number into smaller numbers that total the same, such as: 231 = 100 + 130 + 1.

Perimeter The distance all the way around a 2D shape.

Perpendicular Perpendicular lines are at right angles to each other.

Pictogram A pictogram uses pictures to represent items in a graph. Sometimes one picture represents more than one item – look for the key.

Post meridian After noon. Usually shortened to pm.

Product The result of multiplying two (or more) numbers together.

R

Right angle This is the angle that can be seen in squares.

Roman numerals These can be found on some clocks.

I	II	III	IV	V	VI	VII	VIII	IX	X	XI	XII
1	2	3	4	5	6	7	8	9	10	11	12

S

Standard unit Metric units such as metres, centimetres, grams, kilograms, millilitres, litres, are standard units of measure. Imperial units such as ounces, pounds, yards, feet, inches, pints and gallons are also standard units.

T

Table In statistics a table contains data. For example, how many of each breed there were in a dog show.

V

Vertex The 'point' or 'corner' on a 2D or 3D shape where two straight lines meet.

Vertical A vertical line goes up and down the page

Vertices Plural of 'vertex'.

Notes

Notes

Notes

Multiplication table

x	1	2	3	4	5	6	7	8	9	10	11	12
1	1	2	3	4	5	6	7	8	9	10	11	12
2	2	4	6	8	10	12	14	16	18	20	22	24
3	3	6	9	12	15	18	21	24	27	30	33	36
4	4	8	12	16	20	24	28	32	36	40	44	48
5	5	10	15	20	25	30	35	40	45	50	55	60
6	6	12	18	24	30	36	42	48	54	60	66	72
7	7	14	21	28	35	42	49	56	63	70	77	84
8	8	16	24	32	40	48	56	64	72	80	88	96
9	9	18	27	36	45	54	63	72	81	90	99	108
10	10	20	30	40	50	60	70	80	90	100	110	120
11	11	22	33	44	55	66	77	88	99	110	121	132
12	12	24	36	48	60	72	84	96	108	120	132	144